Green Capitalism

Green Capitalism:
why it can't work

DANIEL TANURO

Resistance Books
IIRE
MERLIN PRESS

First English edition published in 2013 by
The Merlin Press Ltd
99b Wallis Road
London
E9 5LN

www.merlinpress.co.uk

in association with Resistance Books and IIRE
www.resistancebooks.org
www.iire.org

Originally published in French as *L'impossible Capitalisme Vert*
by Editions La Decouverte, Paris, France, 2010

Green Capitalism: why it can't work is issue number 56
of the IIRE Notebooks for Study and Research

© Editions La Decouverte, Paris, France

Edited by Fred Leplat, Kathy Lowe and Dave Kellaway
Translated by Jane Ennis

ISBN. 978-0-85036-646-4

This book is dedicated to Julien, Bruno and Kim

Printed in the UK by Imprint Digital, Exeter

CONTENTS

Acknowledgements	6
Abbreviations	7
Preface to the English edition	9
Introduction	15
Chapter One: Knowledge for decision-making	19
Chapter Two: Why CO_2 is primarily responsible for global warming	22
Chapter Three: The size of the problem	30
Chapter Four: A false consciousness	41
Chapter Five: The necessary and the possible	54
Chapter Six: The double obstacle posed by capitalism	65
Chapter Seven: Kyoto – a haphazard policy	77
Chapter Eight: 'Feet stuck to the accelerator'	85
Chapter Nine: The sorcerers' apprentices	96
Chapter Ten: The destructive dynamic of capitalism?	108
Chapter Eleven: Ecosocialism – the only option	124
Notes	144
About Resistance Books and the IIRE	164

ACKNOWLEDGEMENTS

I am grateful to Michel Husson who has been encouraging me to write this book for several years; to Alfonso Serrano who appeared unexpectedly in my life, offering editorial assistance, and to Jean-Pascal van Ypersele who replied patiently to my questions about the science of climate change. I am especially grateful to Michel Husson for his critical analysis of the first draft of this work. Thanks are also due to Vincent Gay, Jean-Marie Harribey, Pierre Tréfois and my partner Nicole Vandemaele. The responsibility for the final version is obviously mine alone, and I am acutely aware of the unfinished nature of the work. I must also mention various unnamed persons whom I met by chance at conferences, and also several friends whose provocative, unexpected or iconoclastic questions often encouraged me to examine the problems under discussion here from different perspectives.

Daniel Tanuro

ABBREVIATIONS

AEI, American Enterprise Institute
CDM, Clean Development Mechanism
CCS, carbon capture and storage
CO_2, carbon dioxide
ETS, Emission Trading System
IPCC, Intergovernmental Panel on Climate Change
JIM, Joint Implementation Mechanism
FAO, Food and Agriculture Organisation of the United Nations
FEMA, federal Emergency Management Agency
GDP, gross domestic product
NGO, non-governmental organisation
OECD, Organisation for Economic Co-operation and Development
OPEC, Organization of the Petroleum Exporting Countries
OTEC, ocean thermal energy conversion
NASA, National Aeronautics and Space Administration
ULCOS, ultra-low CO_2 steelmaking
UN, United Nations
UNDP, United Nations Development Programme
UNEP, United Nations Environment Programme
UNFCCC, United Nations Framework Convention on Climate Change
UNU-EHS, United Nations University Institute for Environment and Human Security
WTO, World Trade Organisation

PREFACE TO THE ENGLISH EDITION

Most of the French edition of this book, *L'impossible Capitalisme Vert*, was completed in December 2009 since which time many events relevant to the topic have occurred. The Copenhagen climate summit announced a 'green fund' to finance adaptation of developing countries to the effects of global warming. Several countries experienced dramatic floods, unprecedented forest fires or exceptional droughts. A special Intergovernmental Panel on Climate Change (IPCC) report confirmed that the technical potential of renewable energy is more than enough to satisfy the needs of humanity. The Fukushima disaster in Japan reminded the world of the great dangers of nuclear energy. Surveys on the 'carbon bubble' have revealed the motivations of the energy lobby and its interconnection with financial capital. This English edition incorporates these developments.

It is complete on other matters as some inaccuracies have been corrected, and references added. The explanation of the contradictory relationships between human development and environmental change has been expanded. In particular, I have introduced a number of new thoughts and conclusions I have reached in the meantime. These relate to the dialectic in the development of productive forces and the fact that the ecological crisis – the climate crisis particularly – complicates considerably the transition to an ecosocialist society, while making it more urgently needed than ever.[1]

This foreword offers an opportunity to discuss a number of points raised in some debates about the French edition.

Several commentators expressed concern that *L'impossible Capitalisme Vert* focused on the climate and energy challenge. While I do not underestimate other dimensions of environmental degradation my choice is motivated by three considerations. First, the climate crisis encompasses virtually all other aspects of the ecological crisis. Second, the IPCC, as an intergovernmental body, works in such a way that policymakers are confronted directly and inescapably by scientific conclusions that are no longer seriously disputed. Third, the atmospheric saturation by greenhouse gases is the most blatant example of insane mismanagement of the environment which raises the issues of production, consumption and their purposes in a clear and inescapable way.

Certain other readers of the French edition thought that my indictment of capitalism was a bit hasty, because I use the vague concept of 'productivism' and overlook the fact that human development without generalized commodity production would also have come up against the earth's physical limits eventually. This is an interesting discussion, even if it is a bit of political fiction.

Capitalist production is marked by its constant tendency to exceed the needs of the market, which in turn requires it to create new needs. Marx was not afraid to write that capital 'produces to produce,'[2] and that this 'is the trend to boundlessly exceed its own limits'.[3] Thus, from a Marxist point of view, I see no harm in speaking of 'productivism.'

Obviously, this is not to invent a kind of meta-mode of production encompassing capitalism and 'really existing socialism' – because the social relations of production are different and deploy different logics in each case. However, the 'productivism' is a feature of capitalism. For reasons I attempt to analyse here, countries that began to take another path but experienced bureaucratization broke only partially from it.

The capitalist law of population is specific and conditioned by its productivist nature. Maximizing the exploitation of the labour force involves maintaining a relative surplus population to put pressure on wages. In pre-capitalist societies the relative overpopulation was a driver of increased productivity, whereas under capitalism it is the opposite. This reversal has important ecological implications. Danish agricultural economist Ester Boserup has shown that the increase in agricultural productivity in non-capitalist social formations is due to increases in the actual labour per hectare, which allows better management of soil and thus better protection of that resource.[4]

The capitalist increase in agricultural productivity is spectacular and unprecedented, but 'this progress is destructive'[5] because it results from the increased investment in capital in the form of machinery, fertilizers, pesticides and genetically modified organisms, etc. In addition to the ruin of the peasantry, the race for ever-bigger profits leads to monoculture on a large scale, the separation of farming crops and livestock, the hyper-specialization of the two sectors, the standardization of species, the transformation of forests into tree plantations and the radical impoverishment of biotopes. The dialectic of these developments did not escape Marx.[6]

The destructive potential of capitalist productivism stems from the fundamental law of this mode of production, the law of value. An economy that aims for capital accumulation in the abstract form of money cannot spontaneously take into account the destruction of natural resources, since they exist only as concrete use values.

Capital and nature do not speak the same language, and in the words of political economist Joel Kovel[7], one is necessarily the 'enemy' of the other. To pave the way for an alternative, it is not enough to denounce the profit, competition and accumulation: one must go to the root of things, that is to say abolish commodity production and value exchange.

In history, many civilizations that attained a high level of development showed remarkable longevity including China, the Inca Empire, the Mayan Empire and Ancient Egypt whose agricultural system was maintained roughly until the 19th century. This resilience cannot be explained without a proper management of resources, an ability to protect the environment against threats, and even restore it in some cases.[8] Certainly history shows that human induced ecological destruction also occurred. But the current situation of a society so well-informed that it goes straight into the wall, and which still continues to do so, is probably unprecedented (no offence to author Jared Diamond). It seems reasonable to assume that if humanity had not taken the capitalist road it would have been better able to hear signals from the environment and to correct its practices accordingly.

It has been remarked that the book somewhat overstates the possibilities opened up by the technological advances over the last two centuries. A reader pointed out to me that the photovoltaic effect in semiconductor solids could not be exploited without quantum mechanics dating from the 1930s. Moreover, increasing the efficiency of photovoltaic cells needed advanced electronics. Thus, the discovery of the photovoltaic effect in acids by Becquerel in 1839 did not immediately open an energy system alternative to fossil fuels. I bow to that better informed opinion. Nevertheless, the solar thermal (and possibly the fuel cells) could have been exploited since the 19th century and have not been because the monopolies of coal, then oil, did not want it. Above all, I wanted to show that these monopolies have an enormous capacity to influence long-term technological choices and orient research according to their interests. Their nationalization without being bought out or compensated – and that of the credit sector that finances their huge investments – is a prerequisite to any rapid transition to renewables.

I was accused of exaggerating the polemic with the supporters of the 'de-growth' school of thought and I want to dispel any misunderstanding about this. My position on this current can be summarized as follows:

1) The 'de-growth' current has the distinction of having been the first to suggest the need for a reduction of material production (at least in the

developed capitalist countries). The reticence of the different sections of the left to integrate this new constraint is an indicator of their difficulty to break with productivism;

2) The 'de-growth' theory in itself is neither a social project nor a transitional strategy. Its proponents take very different positions with opposed social implications according to their stance on key questions including the relationship between production and consumption, the relative importance of collective action and individual commitment, the strategy relating to the working class struggles, the attitude to power, and the approach to the population issue;

3) There is thus a left and a right wing on the de-growth spectrum. I rank on the right of this movement (though not necessarily on the right of the political spectrum) those who accept the tyranny of experts, focus on the 'educational impact of disasters', consider Malthus as the father of ecology, or put a 'de-growth' gloss on neoliberal austerity measures.

This English edition is published after the Rio+20 UN 2012 Conference on Sustainable Development and the IPCC's Fifth Assessment Report released in September 2013 which focused on the science of climate change. This Report confirms my pessimistic vision, in particular about sea-level rise, undoubtedly the greatest threat from climate shift. According to this document, the temperature rise (compared to pre-industrial period) could be as high as 4,5°C, so that the sea-level could rise by 80 to 90 cm at the end of the 21st century.

But this is not the whole story because the sea level will not stop to rise at the end of the 21st century. According to Anders Levermann, lead author of the sea-level change chapter of the IPCC's Fifth Assessment Report, in the middle term, within a maximum time span of 2000 years, each degree of temperature above the pre-industrial period will unavoidably provoke a sea-level rise of 2.30.* 'Unavoidably' is here the key word. If these projections are right – they are most probably - the future generations will have to face a dramatic and inexorable sea level rise of about 10m, caused by the capitalist quest for the profit. A catastrophe with unimaginable consequences.

While the urgency is greater than it has ever been, Rio+20 like the other conferences, failed to decide anything to protect the earth's resources and climate.

It is possible to satisfy human needs while making the transition to an 'efficient economy'[9] based exclusively on renewable sources. Capitalism cannot do it because this transition requires planning, the sharing of

---

* Anders Levermann, *The inevitability of Sea Level Rise*, http://www.realclimate.org/index.php/archives/2013/08/the-inevitability-of-sea-level-rise/.

resources and knowledge, the cancellation of illegitimate public debts, the relocation of the economy, reducing working hours without loss of pay, the elimination of unnecessary products, and the extension of the public sector and democratic rights .Taken together these measures are inconsistent with the normal functioning of the system. In this sense, Rio+20 confirms that green capitalism is impossible.

Moreover the Rio Summit pledge in favour of a so-called 'green economy' seriously threatens the people and the environment. Indeed, this type of 'green economy' does not aim to respect the ecosystems but to privatize them systematically, so that their 'environmental services' can generate a rent. It is a project based on the neo-liberal dogma that the capitalist ownership of resources ensures their proper management. The UNEP Rio+20[10] report on green economy puts it bluntly: 'Underpricing, mismanagement and, ultimately, the loss of environmental services' result from their 'economic invisibility' that stems from the fact that they are 'primarily public goods and services'.

Will the green economy become the new frontier of accumulation by dispossession, in the words of David Harvey? There are two aspects of this question. On the one hand, the full replacement of the global energy system based on fossil fuels and nuclear energy by a new system based on renewable sources seems at first sight as an opportunity for capital. But, actually, this is a false impression. Firstly, because the condition for this energy transition to be compatible with the struggle against climate change would be to reduce drastically the material production and transportation, in order to compensate for the additional emissions due to the huge investments in the new system. Secondly, because the estimated value of the present global energy system in hands of capital is 15 to 20 trillion dollars, with most infrastructures completely new and recently deployed in emerging countries; as the United Nations World Economic and Social Survey 2011 admits, 'clearly, it is unlikely that the world will decide overnight to write off 15 to 20 trillion dollars in infrastructure and replace it with a renewable energy system having an even higher price tag'. On the other hand, the privatization of resources will not pull capitalism out of its hole. The system's major problem is how to open to growing masses of capital, with an average organic composition tending to increase, fields of valorisation large enough for the 'surplus' value to be realized through the sale of products? Even if the private sector were to totally appropriate forests, freshwaters, oceans, soil, subsoil, atmosphere and the rest, so that all inhabitants of the earth were forced to pay the true cost 'for' environmental services, this re-imposition of the enclosures on a global scale would not provide an answer to the substantive issue, because rent is only a drain on profits coming from the exploitation of wage labour, the only producer of surplus value.

The term 'green economy' is a misnomer for it does not solve the ecological crisis. In the eyes of its neoliberal promoters this kind of economy includes the use of biofuels, nuclear energy and so-called 'clean coal'. Its purpose, as far as its advocates are concerned, is not so much to remove 'dirty' industries as to open up new and safer fields of investment to finance capital shaken by the 2008 crisis. Bankers lay down their conditions, insisting that public authorities must first create the conditions for a sufficient return on their investments. Again, the United Nations Environment Programme (UNEP) report is clear: 'The sectors of finance and investment control trillions of dollars and are able to provide the bulk of funding... But public funding is essential to trigger the transformation of the economy.'

As states are drowning in debt, UNEP calls for 'reforms needed to unlock the job and production potential of a green economy' to act 'as a new engine and not as a retarder of growth.' The measures listed reflect a will to harden neoliberal policies against labour, youth, women, small farmers and indigenous peoples.

This raises the question of who will be the actors in the struggle for an alternative. All social victims of the capitalist system have a role to play. The involvement of critical intellectuals and scientists is also important. But the outcome will depend ultimately on the working class (broadly defined) because, as Francois Chesnais puts it, its daily exploitation potentially positions it against 'the enemy of nature'. The collective struggles of the working class chart a path to a society of associated producers, the only type of society able to break with the reign of commodity production.[11] This strategic dimension – the greening of struggles – should have been amplified in *L'impossible Capitalisme Vert.*

Two centuries after its birth, a diseased capitalism wants to re-impose the enclosures, while pursuing its other social and environmental crimes. That is where the logic of this system that 'exhausts the only two sources of wealth – the earth and the worker' leads us. The intention of this book is to help oppose the logic of capitalism with the ecosocialist logic of the commons, free time and meeting real human needs, democratically determined while respecting our ecosystem.

Daniel Tanuro, July 2013

INTRODUCTION

Three billion human beings live in conditions lacking in human dignity in terms of education, health, energy, water, food, mobility and housing. Their individual needs are modest but in total they are huge – impossible to satisfy without increasing material production. And this in turn means converting resources taken from the environment. Of energy currently consumed, 80% is derived from fossil fuels, the source of greenhouse gases.

At the same time 200 years of 'productivism' have brought the climate system to the brink of collapse. In certain areas – small island states, the Arctic regions, the arid zones, mountain valleys where the water flow is disrupted by melting glaciers – the tipping point has already been reached. In order to prevent climate change spiralling out of control and affecting hundreds of millions of people, greenhouse gas emissions must be drastically reduced. But currently consumption of fossil fuel is necessary in order to convert resources derived from the environment – hence material production.

How can the climate be stabilised while the legitimate rights to development are recognised of those who have nothing, or very little, and who are at the same time the main victims of global warming? This is the problem of the century.

According to neo-liberal governments and big business, the market economy can solve the problem. The solution, they say, is not to slow down the economic machine but to revive it. In order to reduce carbon emissions to manageable proportions all that is needed is to put a prohibitive price on carbon. The economies of the Global South could promote the protection of their forests, sell the right to pollute and export biomass. With the proceeds they could then buy technologies appropriate to businesses from the North, which would reduce unemployment in developed countries...

In reality, the virtues of this market approach exist only in the imagination of its creators.

Firstly, the argument is weakened at the outset because the powerful fossil fuel lobbies and the sectors which depend on them refuse to pay the bill. Although the monopolies have been forced to admit the necessity of a reduction in the output of oil they are demanding to be allowed to organise this as they see fit, at a speed of their choice and while maintaining control of energy production in order to protect their enormous profits. But this demand is incompatible with the need for a very rapid transition. With all due respect to the emulators of Adam Smith, meeting the deadline set by climate science is impossible unless the investment – essential to the formation of a new, efficient energy system, based on renewables – is planned without reference to the costs.

Secondly, changing a source of energy is not enough in itself. A new system of production and distribution is needed. It would require huge investments to set up the new system and that system would generate supplementary emissions which would have to be offset by a reduction of activity in other sectors. In other words, production would have to be reduced and fewer goods produced and transported.

It is impossible to meet this challenge within the framework of a mode of production in which each investor is seeking to replace workers with machines which improve labour productivity, in order to gain an advantage over the competition. Productivism is inherent in capitalism. The system's bulimic consumption of energy derives from its logic of unlimited accumulation, which is the main cause of the ecological crisis and the climate crisis.

The problem is structural and therefore the solution is very far from being a technological one. Admittedly, the practical challenges to be met are very complex, but there is no reason to believe that the problems are insoluble. Energy reserves are considerable and the technological potential of renewables would meet the demands of humanity ten times over. The impasse is therefore social, not physical. The basis of the problem is political. In the final analysis the choice we are faced with is dramatically simple.

We can create a different type of society in which capitalist production is drastically reduced and thereby impose maximum limits on the damage caused by global warming while guaranteeing a quality of life for everyone based exclusively on renewable energy. Alternatively we can continue with the capitalist logic of more and more frenetic accumulation. The climate change resulting from this will drastically limit the rights to existence of millions of people and future generations will be condemned to deal with the problems created by dangerous technologies: nuclear, biofuels, genetically modified organisms, tar sands and carbon capture and storage.

Bogged down in its own contradictions, incapable of renewing itself as in the growth period of the post-war boom and faced with the physical limits of the earth's resources, the capitalist system is in a dead end. At the same time, it is holding a sword of Damocles over the heads of vast numbers of women and men, most of whom have an insignificant responsibility for the climate crisis. This sums up the current situation.

Twenty years after political scientist Francis Fukuyama expressed the belief that it was possible to announce the end of history, an alternative is more necessary than ever. It hardly suffices to say that the challenge is great. It is a Herculean task. Far-reaching structural changes are essential involving not only redistribution of wealth but, more fundamentally, a re-definition of social wealth.

What goods and services do we need? What should we produce? How and in what quantities? Who decides? These questions were already being asked in the 19th century by British artist, writer and socialist William Morris.

Now we can add others. What sort of environment do we want to live in? How can we 'listen' to nature when considering the impact of our choices? What will the consequences of these choices be? How will we manage them? And what chance will we have to change course if it turns out that we were mistaken? In the final analysis, the response to these decisive questions always comes up against the same obstacle; the freedom for capitalists in competition with each other to invest and produce more and more, where they want, when they want, how they want, in the interest of profit. Quite simply they want to force-feed those who have the means to become 'consumers' and let everyone else go hang.

The necessary alternative is not merely political in the current sense of the term. We must decide what kind of civilisation we want.

Gurus spread panic in the hope of putting a Green spin, without anyone noticing, on the theory of population growth developed by British scholar Thomas Malthus. They are only too happy to attribute global warming to so-called over population and a worrying number of them seem to find it easier to challenge the right of part of humanity to exist than to challenge capitalism. They should not be underestimated with their reactionary rantings, as they are beating a path to the highest levels of the ruling class. There is no need to look for a conspiracy: capitalism itself points the way to barbarism.

Urgently needed are a left-looking ecology, a socialist ecology and an 'ecosocialist' approach. And this book aims to assist the Left along this road. My starting point is the idea that there can no longer be a radical project for changing society that fails to take into account the limits and constraints imposed by nature. Environmental problems are now inseparable from social problems. Climate change obliges us to acknowledge that people determine their own social and local environment *and* the global environment. From now on, we have the responsibility of deciding not only the society we want – or do not want – for our descendants, but also what sort of natural world. It is therefore not enough to add an ecological chapter to the programme for a different society. It is not sufficient to add a chapter on ecology to the programme for another society. The limit to quantitative development is not in a distant future, but is in front of us today, as an essential *aggiornamento.*

The ecological question determines both the alternative and the steps to be taken to achieve that alternative. We need urgently to devise a strategy, no matter how difficult, for uniting social campaigns and ecological campaigns. This requires a radical approach since capitalism involves the appropriation of natural resources and once these are in the hands of the owners of capital, the result tends to be the ruthless exploitation of the resources and of those working with them.

The 19th and 20th centuries were dominated by the 'socialist question'. The 21st will be dominated by the new 'ecosocialist' question. Only a Left that challenges capitalism can initiate a valid response. But there are conditions to be fulfilled. Scientific confidence must give way to caution. Dreams of domination over nature must give way to a collective sense of responsibility that is both benevolent and alert.

Even the concept of liberty cannot avoid re-examination since accepting natural limits and respecting the rhythms and cycles of the ecology of the planet ultimately means accepting limits on the emancipation from work and on the increase productivity. There is no other choice but to accept restrictions to freedoms. If the Left tries to evade this responsibility, it would be betraying the hundreds of millions of poor people who are already suffering the effects of global warming and would also be betraying and misunderstanding Karl Marx. When Marx analysed soil depletion during the Industrial Revolution, he concluded with a warning: 'The only possible freedom is that social man, the associated producers, rationally regulate their exchange of matter with nature'.

This book was first published in French at the time of the UN Climate Summit in Copenhagen, December 2009. In spite of the urgency, the signing of a new, binding international treaty was postponed. Governments have other priorities. Having saved the banks at great expense they now intend, with impeccable neo-liberal logic, to shift the burden of the deficit onto the public. In any case the agreement they would have signed, and which they probably will sign one day, would have been disgraceful – ecologically inadequate, socially criminal and technologically dangerous.

Different policies are necessary. Another world and another climate are possible. But they can only come from social mobilisations.

Chapter One
KNOWLEDGE FOR DECISION-MAKING

The Left is rightly wary of the forays of 'science' into politics. It is suspicious of a dictatorship which eliminates democratic debate and gives an appearance of objectivity to back up the imperatives of those in power. The most radical left critics look askance at the Intergovernmental Panel on Climate Change (IPCC). According to them this official organ of university professors, set up by the United Nations, can only be an instrument of the established order. Indeed, the *Summaries for Decision Makers* has been adopted by many governments.[12]

For some the IPCC exaggerates in order to alarm the populace and make them willing to accept sacrifices, but others think that it under-estimates the gravity of global warming in an attempt to minimize the responsibility of capitalism.

Both scepticism and exaggeration express suspicion of an establishment science. Now, it is as well to put things in perspective. The IPCC consists of three working groups – climate science, impact of climate change, and methods of reducing emissions – which evaluate and synthesise publications appearing in peer-reviewed journals. Group III is full of economists who synthesise the work of their colleagues world-wide. The vast majority of the articles reviewed are neo-liberal in tone, for the simple reason that there are very few critical economists in the academic world. The reports emanating from this group are questionable from a social point of view, as they are based on the notion of 'cost efficiency'.[13] In response, this book will argue the opposite – the case for resisting climate change by all possible means, regardless of cost, and for social and technological reasons. This mixture of political debate and scientific controversy is typical of human sciences, in which several rival 'paradigms' co-exist, according to Thomas Kuhn.[14]

Groups I and II are a different case. Group I, devoted to climate science, is based exclusively on Natural Sciences, therefore on a rigorously established body of knowledge, verified time and time again. In periods of normality, outside what Kuhn calls 'scientific revolutions', this body of knowledge is rightly considered the sole framework for understanding the real world.

Group II, studying impact and adaptation, is based on Human Sciences, in particular on four possible scenarios for human development elaborated by Group III. The scenarios certainly do not cover the entire range of possibilities but they do not make capitalism more attractive.

In general terms, since the procedures for peer review are very stringent, these two Groups may be considered to have produced an excellent synthesis of 'good science'.

It is undeniable that this 'good science' is subject to intense pressure. The January 2007 Paris conference on the Fourth IPCC report brought to light the extent to which certain governments and commercial concerns have tried to influence climate research and the methods used, both directly and indirectly. A dossier completed by an American scientific association, based on the examination of hundreds of specific cases, has revealed 'the numerous ways in which American climate science has been filtered, weakened and manipulated in the course of the last five years'.[15]

Sharon Hays, leader of the US delegation to the conference, admitted candidly that government officials in office at the time had done all they could – successfully – to ensure that the report toned down the relationship between global warming and cyclones.[16] It was a question of ensuring that the damage caused in the US by Hurricane Katrina, which had devastated New Orleans less than two years previously, would not be attributed too incontrovertibly to the climate policies of the Bush administration. The American Enterprise Institute (AEI), a lobby group financed by ExxonMobil, offered scientists and economists 10,000 dollars each to write articles undermining the credibility of the Fourth IPCC report.[17]

Nevertheless the story of this dossier is of 'good science' fighting against 'state-controlled science'. We cannot underestimate how long and difficult this fight has been. The first warnings against the risks of global warming date back to a 1957 report by two American oceanographers, Revell and Suess.[18] The observatory at Mauna Loa (Hawaii) was founded in 1958. As soon as it became operational it confirmed the accelerated accumulation greenhouse gases in the atmosphere.

But politicians dragged their feet. More than 20 years were to elapse before the UN convened the first World Conference on Climate (Geneva 1979) and more than 30 years before the IPCC was formed. Scientific researchers, however, acted with remarkable speed. Barely two years after its foundation the IPCC produced its first evaluation report (Geneva, 1990) with conclusions that have essentially been confirmed by three subsequent reports. Although they were at first disputed, especially by the US which blocked the dossier for some time, they were accepted in the end.

The Bali conference of 2008 was a defeat for the line taken by US President George W Bush. Subsequently the election of Barak Obama as President reduced the ability of climate change deniers to interfere with the message that scientists were sending to the politicians. Nevertheless, these climate change deniers have not admitted defeat. The problem of climate change is far from having been resolved, but no responsible person can now deny there is a problem and that it must be resolved. In spite of considerable political and economic pressure, climatologists have succeeded in exposing the 'inconvenient truth'.

Rather than splitting hairs over the reliability of the IPCC projections, the Left should seize upon this 'fact' (scientist do not hold the 'truth'), translate it into social terms and call upon the researchers who have discovered it to decide which side they are on.

In fact it is not just a question of pure science. The philosopher Ernst Bloch, author of *The Principle of Hope*, called it 'knowledge indispensable for decision-making'. Bloch said that such knowledge could not be contemplative as it was 'linked to the evolutionary process' and must therefore 'actively take the side of Good... that which upholds human dignity in its procedure'. For him this method of undertaking research could even be 'the only objective one, the only one which reflects the reality of history ... elaborated by human endeavour'. Bloch concludes, 'From the very fact that it is no longer merely contemplative, such a scientific method calls upon the active producers of history'.

These lines could have been written expressly with climate change in mind. But climate change introduces a new dimension for it is clear that the creation of history also involves what happens to the environment both locally and globally. Now we see that human beings are just as much responsible for creating the climate crisis as the world economic crisis. Unless this is understood and acted upon, the project of a world free of exploitation or oppression has no chance of success.

Chapter Two
WHY CO_2 IS PRIMARILY RESPONSIBLE FOR GLOBAL WARMING

The Ancient Philosophers said that all is in continual flux. This includes carbon which, like all the elements, is present on the earth in finite quantities and in different chemical combinations. It is found in four major locations; the atmosphere, the biosphere (the mass of living organisms whose molecules are built around carbon atoms), the hydrosphere (water, especially the oceans), and the lithosphere (certain rocks containing enormous quantities of carbon). Carbon circulates continually between these locations, combining with different elements.

In the atmosphere carbon is essentially present in the form of carbon dioxide. The particular quality of carbon dioxide (CO_2) is that it is in effect the original source of the growth of green plants. They absorb it through their stomata and, thanks to their own chlorophyll and to solar energy, combine it with water to synthesise more complex, organic molecules. Only green plants have this incredible capacity to photosynthesize, which makes them into the base of the pyramid of living organisms.

However, vegetation does not only absorb CO_2 but also disposes of it through transpiration, a form of combustion. And any combustion of material containing carbon results on the one hand in a release of energy in the form of heat and on the other in a release of carbon dioxide. During its growth to maturity, a plant absorbs more CO_2 by photosynthesis than it releases through respiration. When it matures, the two processes are in equilibrium.

As the plant withers, the emissions prevail over the absorptions. Finally, it dies and decomposes, that is to say, the large organic molecules are broken up into smaller and smaller molecules by the actions of an army of insects, worms, bacteria and fungi. Thanks to these 'reductive organisms', most of the carbon returns to the atmosphere in the form of CO_2 or methane, a gas which reacts with the oxygen in the air to produce CO_2 and water vapour.

Everything is in flux everywhere. The exchange of matter with the atmosphere does not happen only on *terra firma* but in water, particularly in the oceans which cover the major part of the globe. In the same way as green terrestrial plants, algae and vegetable plankton (phytoplankton) absorb and discharge large quantities of CO_2.

But this is not the only, or even the principal way, in which liquid environments form part of the exchange of matter with the atmosphere. Atmospheric CO_2 dissolves in water, and this purely physical dissolution is considerably more significant because water is cold. It is an important characteristic as it unites the circulation of carbon to the continual movement of the oceans, known as thermohaline circulation.

Water is also in ceaseless flux. The surface of the sea freezes close to the poles. This means that free bodies of water become more saline and thus denser, which in turn means that they are drawn towards the ocean depths. They are replaced on the surface by other liquid masses from further south. This huge and natural thermosyphon originating in the Polar Regions is the origin of the great marine currents like the Gulf Stream which function as a continuous loop on a global scale.

Thanks to their lower temperature, the seas of the colder regions dissolve larger quantities of CO_2. When they go beneath the surface, the waters therefore remove larger quantities of carbon. When they have completed half their loop they return to the surface and are warmed by the tropical sun, releasing part of the carbon they contain in the form of carbon dioxide (a process known as degassing). Then these same bodies of water complete their circuit by returning to the north to replace the colder waters which have gone beneath the surface in their turn, containing dissolved carbon. And so on...

There is a continual flux of carbon through the atmosphere, biosphere and hydrosphere. This applies also to the lithosphere. On the surface, eroded rocks release calcium and compounds containing carbon – carbonates. Rivers take calcium and carbonates to the oceans where all sorts of organisms make use of them to build calcareous shells, based on calcium carbonate. When these organisms die they sink to the bottom of the sea. In the depths they hardly decompose at all, so the carbon they contain is not released as gas but accumulates and gradually builds up enormous stocks of matter.

Nevertheless, on a geological time-scale, neither is the magma static. Rather, just like water in a saucepan, it is moved by convection currents which appear on the surface of the earth in a process known to geologists as the movement of the tectonic plate. These movements are obviously extremely slow but when one under-water plate slips beneath another (causing an earthquake or even a tsunami) the reserves of carbon at the bottom of the sea are drawn to the depths of the earth where they are subjected to extreme pressures and high temperatures. The organic part (the 'corpses' of the micro-organisms) turn into petroleum, carbon and natural gas, while the inorganic part (shells) gives rise to other rock formations, known as carbonates (limestone, marble, etc.)

Thanks to the currents at the core of the magma, rocks formed in the depths are eventually pushed up to the surface where modification and erosion again release calcium and carbonates. Carbon can also be returned to the atmosphere during volcanic eruptions which release very large quantities of CO_2 and equally significant amounts of sulphur. Sulphur particles in suspension – aerosols – play an important role in the climate as they reflect the sun's rays into space and thus tend to temporarily cool the lower atmosphere.

These phenomena not only concern marine sediments but also organic debris accumulated on dry land. Indeed, only a very small portion of the inert terrestrial biomass escapes the process of reduction. Instead of returning to the atmosphere as CO_2 or methane, its carbon is stored in the ground in the form of organic matter. In the long term, this too can be drawn into the depths.

These exchanges are known as the 'carbon cycle'. To simplify, it could be said that the cycle consists of three related and interconnected loops; an atmosphere-biosphere loop in which relatively small quantities of carbon circulate rapidly; an atmosphere-hydrosphere loop in which larger quantities of carbon take up to a thousand years to circulate; and a biosphere-hydrosphere-lithosphere loop, in which millions of gigatonnes of carbon take tens or hundreds of millions of years to circulate.

What is the link between these processes and climate change? Along with some other gases (methane, nitrous oxide, water vapour ...)[19] carbon dioxide has the property of letting pass the rays of the to the earth while limiting the escape of infra-red rays from earth to space. In other words this gas fills the role of the panes of glass which retain heat in a greenhouse; hence the expression 'greenhouse effect'.

The physical explanation of this asymmetry lies in the fact that the two types of radiation have different wavelengths. Unlike incidental rays, infra-red rays heat molecules of CO_2 that they encounter so the molecules in their turn emit infra-red rays in all directions. Because of this the earth, warmed by the sun, does not discharge all this thermal energy into space and some of it remains in the lower atmosphere, heating the surface of the globe. In itself this 'greenhouse effect' is beneficial. Without it the median temperature of our planet would be 17°C below zero, whereas thanks to it the median temperature is 15°C above zero.

Our climate differs in many ways from that of the other planets in the solar system. Not only is the temperature mild, it is also relatively stable. Solar radiation is 30% greater than it was three and a half billion years ago, but the median temperature of our good old earth is very far from having altered to the same extent.[20] This relative stability is the result of a whole series of complex mechanisms which regulate the concentration of carbon in the atmosphere, some of them linked to the very existence of life and the biosphere.

When the concentration of CO_2 in the atmosphere increases for one reason or another, for example when an increase in the period of natural sunlight causes a warming of the oceans and thus a significant degassing, green plants grow more quickly. In this way they take in carbon from the atmosphere and slow down excessive warming to a certain extent. There are other even more subtle regulatory mechanisms but it would be too much of a digression to describe them here.[21] The key point to bear in mind is that, under normal conditions, the exchanges of carbon between the reservoirs tend to stabilise themselves, and thus the temperature of the earth is relatively stable. This has been the case since green plants covered the surface of the earth and created an atmosphere similar to ours today. It led James Lovelock to propound his Gaia hypothesis that everything happens as though life on earth were preserving the conditions for its own survival.[22]

The history of the earth is also the history of climates. We have a relatively precise idea of this history thanks to analysis of air-bubbles trapped in ancient ice which enables us to determine the composition of the atmosphere in remote periods of the past. This analysis makes it possible to trace the evolutionary curves of the concentration of carbon in the atmosphere (CO_2 and CH_4[23]) according to the era. Examination of these evolutionary curves reveals that the quantity of greenhouse gases in the atmosphere has fluctuated in a remarkably regular manner within a fairly narrow range. Looking back to 400,000 years ago we can clearly distinguish four periods when there was less carbon in the atmosphere. Geological and paleontological data confirm that these periods correspond to the four glaciations of the quaternary era.

A closer examination of the graphs reveals that, at the beginning of each inter-glacial period, the rise in temperature occurred shortly before the increase in atmospheric concentration of carbon. The alternation of glacial and inter-glacial periods over these 400,000 years is therefore not due in the first instance to variations in the quantity of greenhouse gases in the atmosphere. So what did cause it? The answer lies in natural modifications of the amount of sunlight resulting from various periodic changes to the position of the earth relative to the sun. (The form of the terrestrial ellipse, the tilt of the earth's axis, and the point of the ellipse where the earth is located when it is at the equinox, vary regularly over the course of time).

During periods of glaciation resulting from a smaller amount of sunlight, the concentration of CO_2 in the atmosphere is reduced because the oceans cool down, and cold water dissolves much more CO_2 than warm water does. In other words, during the history of the earth, every period of cooling due to reduced amount of sunlight has been accentuated by the reduction of greenhouse gases due to CO_2 dissolving in cooler oceans.

Specialists use the term 'climatic feedback' to describe processes of this nature. They distinguish between positive feedback – which intensifies the initial phenomenon – and negative feedback which contradicts it. Another example of positive feedback is when, during a glacial period, a large area of the globe is covered in snow and ice and these vast white expanses considerably reduce the warming of the surface of the earth by reflecting more radiation into space (a process known as augmentation of the albedo).

The natural climate changes of the past have had considerable effects in many areas. During glacial periods, since precipitation in the form of snow was considerable and since a large amount of this snow did not melt in the summer and accumulated in the form of glaciers, the level of the oceans was reduced.

Conversely during inter-glacial periods, the temperature rose, the ice retreated, the sea level rose and the temperature of the oceans increased. The CO_2 released by the oceans intensified the greenhouse effect, vegetation developed more quickly, tending to absorb more CO_2, and the reflection of radiation (albedo) diminished. It should be noted that, during the alternation between glacial and inter-glacial periods, although the conditions of life on earth changed radically between one period and the next, variations in temperature remained fairly limited. For example, at the end of the last Ice Age 20,000 years ago, the median temperature was only 4.5°C lower than present day temperatures.

This has been a very cursory summary of extremely complex, slow modifications, extending over many tens of thousands of years. At times the process has been accelerated, but this has always been the result of very gradual, cumulative processes in the course of which, little by little, quantity was preparing to become quality.

The relative stability of the terrestrial climate and the slow pace of change in the composition of the atmosphere are two aspects in which the current situation differs sharply from the past. Indeed, if we extend the graph of carbon concentrations in the atmosphere in relation to time, we can see quite clearly that the present day is characterised by a strong, severe increase. The quantity of carbon dioxide and methane in the atmosphere today is almost twice as high as the average during the inter-glacial periods of 800,000 years ago. The expression 'climate change' is in fact ill-chosen because it suggests a gradual change, similar to those which the earth has experienced in the course of its long history, yet this far from being the case. It would be more accurate to use the term 'climate shift' to describe the current situation.

When this shift is compared with past climate changes it will be noted that the chain of causation is different. This point is decisive for the refutation of climate change deniers who rely in particular on the nature of previous glacial periods in order to call into question the driving force of CO_2 in the current situation.[24] As we have seen during inter-glacial periods in the past, greater amounts of sunlight gave rise to an increase in temperatures which resulted in an increase in the concentration of carbon in the atmosphere, which in turn led to an increase in the greenhouse effect and thus an additional rise in temperature. The situation we are confronted with today does not correspond with this three-stage schema.

According to research in astrophysics, variations in amount of sunlight and solar activity only account for between 5% and 10% of global warming.[25] The rest stems directly from the increase in the greenhouse effect caused by the rise in concentration of carbon in the atmosphere. To simplify, it could be said that in the past climate change caused the increase in the greenhouse effect. Today it is the increase in the greenhouse effect which directly gives rise to climate change or, to be more exact, climate shift.

Every year the scientists who follow the development of atmospheric composition from observatories such as Mona Loa in Hawaii publish charts demonstrating an increasingly rapid rise in the quantity of carbon in the atmosphere. Logically, this increase is mirrored by an increase in climate change.

Other scientists worldwide are reporting a whole series of phenomena consistent with this increase in the greenhouse effect. The mean surface temperature is increasing more and more rapidly (0.8°C since 1850); plant and animal species are migrating in the attempt to find habitats adapted to their needs; glaciers and snow-covered surfaces are obviously retreating, sometimes quite spectacularly, in almost every region of the earth the temperature of the oceans is rising, so that their mass is expanding and sea-levels are rising (10-20 cm during the 20th century). Cyclones are becoming increasingly violent and extreme meteorological events are becoming more frequent.

All these changes, and many others, are well-documented. There is no longer any doubt that the primary cause of these changes is the increase of carbon concentration in the atmosphere – in other words, in the increase of the temperature of the surface of the earth.

What are the causes of these increased quantities of carbon in the atmosphere? One is deforestation – quite understandable in view of what has been said above about the carbon cycle. If trees are felled and not replaced and if the acreage occupied by forests is reduced, the reservoirs where the carbon is stored as organic matter are also destroyed. (This is why the expression 'carbon sinks' is used to describe forests and oceans).

It is true that carbon storage can continue for a period in partial form, for example in the form of wood products, but once this wood is burnt, the carbon will be released in the form of CO_2. Furthermore, the forest reservoirs of carbon are not formed solely of tree-trunks. The canopies and roots of trees store large quantities of organic matter, as does humus. When the canopy is burnt, the roots decay, and soil which is cultivated or turned into pasture loses a significant amount of its humus.

However, the major cause of the increase of carbon concentration in the atmosphere is the combustion of coal, oil and natural gas. Here also the basic information about the carbon cycle is relevant. These fuels are known as 'fossil fuels' because they originate in a biomass that has been dead for hundreds of millions of years, and which has been concentrated but which has not decomposed. The biomass has fossilised in the bowels of the earth and released methane (which explains the presence of natural gas close to deposits of oil and coal).

The practical use of this fossilised biomass for humanity is obvious for it has a significantly higher energy content than other resources such as wood. Oil has the further advantage of existing in liquid form, which makes it a very convenient source of energy, especially for transport. Unfortunately, burning this fossilised biomass extracted from the bowels of the earth causes a kind of short-circuit in the long loop of the carbon cycle, which passes through the lithosphere and extends over hundreds of millions of years.

In other words, burning the fossilised biomass injects into the atmosphere quantities of carbon that could exceed the absorptive ability of green plants and of the oceans. The global economy currently emits six gigatonnes of carbon from the use of fossil fuels and almost two gigatonnes from deforestation.[26] This is double what the 'sink' can absorb. In other words, the short loop of the carbon cycle, which passes through the biosphere, the atmosphere and the hydrosphere, is saturated with the mass of carbon which we emit (derived largely from the long loop) to satisfy our demands for energy.

Global warming is an inevitable result of this saturation. We, *Homo sapiens*, the thinking matter, the most sophisticated form developed by life, are modifying the Earth's climate that the life contributed to regulate. This change in climate will, if unchecked, lead to dramatic changes to our physical environment. It may seem unbelievable that we, tiny human ants, could have such a global impact on our huge planet. But the fact is that, apart from water vapour, the other gases which can lead to changes to the green house effect are present in the atmosphere in infinitesimally small quantities.

Atmospheric concentration of CO_2 is expressed in terms of parts per million (abbreviated to ppm). Three hundred parts of carbon dioxide per million (300ppm CO_2) means that, for every million molecules present in a given volume of air, hardly 300 are molecules of CO_2. Methane is even rarer, measured in parts per billion. Since the quantities of fossil carbon occurring in the lithosphere are much higher than those present in the atmosphere (seven million gigatonnes as opposed to 750 gigatonnes), and given that CO_2 continues to survive in the atmosphere for about 150 years,[27] clearly we are on the point of profoundly changing the climate of our world, or even drastically disrupting it. All we need to do is to burn fossil carbon quickly enough and that is exactly what we are doing.

Chapter Three
THE SIZE OF THE PROBLEM

The Swedish physicist Svante August Arrhenius (1859-1927) was the first scientist to propose the hypothesis of climate change caused by the use of fossil fuels. His estimate of a 5°C rise in temperature by the end of the 20th century was reasonably close to that proposed today by climatologists.[28] Arrhenius wished to believe that this phenomenon would have positive benefits for humanity but we now know that this is not the case. The disadvantages outweigh the advantages, even with a limited rise in temperatures, and it is most probable that the phenomenon will reach highly dangerous levels.

The 2007 IPCC report presents a chart which indicates that a rise in temperature of between 0.6 and 5°C during the 21st century, there will be negative impacts with an 80% probability of occurring. These impacts are indentified in five key areas; access to fresh water, ecosystems (especially biodiversity), food production, coastal zones (entire communities obliged to relocate because of a rise in sea levels and salinisation of aquifers), and human health. In the following pages, this chart will be referred to as The Impact Chart. Its significance derives not only from the fact that it is very wide-ranging, but also from the fact that it has been integrated into the *Summary for Decision Makers.*[29]

Every evaluation report by the IPCC is the subject, not only of a technical summary, but also of a summary addressed to decision makers. The distinctive feature of this document is that every word in it has been discussed, on the one hand by the scientists responsible for the complete report, and on the other by government representatives. In the final analysis its formal endorsement involves governments.

No holder of political office can ever claim they didn't know what appears in these documents. They can't claim they didn't know. It is already known that the rate of morbidity and mortality increases during heat waves, floods and droughts. Health care systems are already coping with an increased burden because of climate change. This burden will become a heavy one with a rise of 2°C

The areas of distribution of disease-bearing insects are already increasing. Anopheles mosquitoes transmit malaria to the highlands of Kenya where it was previously absent. Sheep ticks transmit Lyme disease[30] as far north as Sweden of Arrhenius where they are now resistant to mild winters. The increase in temperature is already leading in many regions to a reduction in the harvest of small farmers and in the catch of small-scale fishing businesses, which provide the means of subsistence for the local population.

Even a minimal increase in temperature leads to increased water shortages for hundreds of millions of people. An increase of 1°C in the 21st century would lead to intensified drought in sub-tropical regions and a decrease in the productivity of certain cereal crops in semi-arid tropical regions. In the event of an increase of 2°C, millions more people each year would be subjected to coastal flooding. In the event of a rise of 3.5°C, there would be widespread reduction of agricultural productivity for all cereal crops, in all latitudes.

Inevitably, the chart is not comprehensive. With reference to agricultural resources, for example, productive potential in developed countries could increase by 8% by 2080, whereas that of developing countries could fall by 9%. The global deficit seems minimal, but the details, region by region, are more worrying. Latin America and Africa would be the worst affected continents, with loss of productivity of over 12%, perhaps even 15%.

In certain regions of sub-Saharan Africa, the productivity of land that is not irrigated could even drop by 50% in the next 20 years.[31] According to the UN Food and Agriculture Organisation of, 'In around forty poor countries, with a population of two billion, of whom 450 million suffer from famine, loss of agricultural production resulting from climate change would dramatically increase the number of people suffering from malnutrition.'

The FAO confirms that Sub-Saharan Africa would suffer the most. It estimates that the arid lands where the growth period of crops is less than 120 days covers 1.1 billion hectares and considers that aridity in this region could increase from 5% - 8% between now and 2080. Outside of Africa, all tropical and sub-tropical regions could be affected. Cereal production in 65 countries, where more than half the population of the developing world lives, is at risk of falling by about 280 million tonnes (about 16% of the agricultural GDP of these countries).[32]

How many people are threatened? The Impact Chart only gives a few indications, but numerous estimates are available. In the first instance, the impact obviously depends upon the scope of global warming. The mid-point on the scale of IPCC projections would suggest increase in global warming of more than 3.5°C in relation to the pre-industrial period or about 2.8°C compared to the 21st century. Some researchers estimate that this would mean coastal floods could affect between 100 and 150 million people between now and 2050, famine could hit up to 600 million, and malaria 300 million, while water shortages could involve as many as three billion more people.[33]

These estimates are evidently subject to uncertainty.[34] Furthermore, the impacts vary according to social factors which can to some extent increase or diminish them, especially if increases in temperature are limited. The damage caused by malaria, for instance, is not inevitable since it is directly linked to poverty and under-development. The fact remains that if the political situation does not change the general scope of these threats is considerable.

The majority of victims are found in poor countries and this will continue to be the case if things do not change. Statistics on susceptibility to climate crises – not necessarily global warming – give an indication. Between 2000 and 2004, about 262 million people every year were affected by meteorological disasters and 98% of them lived in 'developing countries'. While the proportion of victims in 'developed countries' (members of the OECD) was one in 1,500, it was one in 19 in the developing world – 79 times greater.[35]

The majority of people in danger of having to re-locate between now and 2050 as a result of the rise in sea levels live in the Global South where the infrastructures for protection are inadequate. Estimates according to country illustrate the scale of the problem; 30 million Chinese, 30 million Indians, 15-20 million Bengalis, 10-14 million Egyptians and 10 million inhabitants of other large deltas such as the Niger, would be at risk. On a comparatively smaller scale, but particularly tragic, is the case of small island states such as Tuvalu or the Maldives, which will most probably just cease to exist within the next 50 years. Furthermore, 50 million people could be driven from places rendered uninhabitable due to damage caused by the rise in water levels.[36]

It is the poor who are most at risk. They lack resources which would enable them to adapt to climate change. High rents or homelessness force them to settle, sometimes illegally, in areas such as flood plains or steep hillsides – precisely the kind of locations susceptible to landslips or mudslides during heavy rainfall. The poor living there have no means of escape in case of catastrophe or are afraid to flee for fear of not being able to return and of losing what little they have. And governments all too often do not care about their fate...

Widespread in the Global South these disasters where (with the notable exception of Cuba) the poor are left to fend for themselves are not unknown in 'developed countries' either. In Louisiana in 2005, Hurricane Katrina caused the loss of 1,500 lives and left 780,000 people without homes. 750,000 of these had no form of insurance.

In the absence of any evacuation procedures undertaken by the municipal authorities, 138,000 of the 480,000 inhabitants of New Orleans were trapped[37], left waiting for rescue without drinking water, electricity or telephone communication for five days. The vast majority of them were low-paid workers or unemployed, children of poor families and elderly people without means of support. 28% of the population of New Orleans is poor (the US average is 12%) and 35% of the African-American inhabitants are poor (the US average is 25%): their districts were the worst affected, 75% of the population in the flooded areas was African-American. Among the poor, women, children and the elderly suffered most.

Similar disasters are not unknown in Europe. The heat wave of 2003 caused more than 30,000 deaths. Which makes it after the Chernobyl nuclear accident, one of the most significant ecological catastrophes of our time in 'developed countries'.

In the UK 1.6 million people live in areas at high risk of flooding with working-class areas particularly at risk. *Future Flooding*, a report issued in 2004 by the UK government's Office of Science and Technology, expresses the fear that climate change may increase the danger to 'unacceptable' levels: 2.6 to 3.6 million people at risk by 2080. These figures only refer to floods caused by a rise in sea levels and increased rainfall.

The impact of what the report calls urban flooding should also be taken into account – flooding due to short but heavy bursts of rainfall which exceed the absorptive capacity of sewage and drainage systems. Frequently underestimated in risk evaluation, these floods are significant in public health terms, since rainwater gets mixed up with sewage and industrial waste, causing problems of pollution. According to *Future Flooding*, the number of people in the UK exposed to the risks of urban flooding could rise from the current figure of 200,000 to 700,000 or even 900,000 by 2080. The report states that 'socially disadvantaged people will be most adversely affected', since 'the poor are less able to take out insurance against floods or to pay for the damage'.

Generally speaking, socially disadvantaged persons in all regions of the world are above all women, who constitute 80% of the 1.3 billion human beings living below the poverty threshold. Furthermore, women are specifically affected as a result of their specific oppression. In less developed countries, they are faced with the heavy burden of collecting firewood and also with the reduction of income from agriculture, two areas of work which most often fall to women. In more developed countries, lack of job security and low salaries affect women in particular, leaving them with access to fewer resources for protection against global warming.

It is advisable to evaluate not only the immediate effects and the cost of any possible environmental catastrophe, but also the medium-term consequences for the dynamics of development of societies. A climatic accident can have a whole series of consequences. *Future Flooding* notes the significance of syndromes of deep depression among victims of repeated flooding and the resulting costs for social security systems.

These medium-term repercussions are particularly worrying in the poorest regions. In Ethiopia and Kenya, two of the countries most at risk of drought, the probability that children under five will suffer from malnutrition is 36-50% greater if they are born during a drought. In Ethiopia in 2005 the drought factor resulted in an increase of almost two million in the number of children suffering from malnutrition. In Niger, the risk of children under two suffering from stunted growth increases by 72% for those born during a drought. The opportunity for Indian women to go to primary school was reduced by 19% after the floods in the 1970s.[38]

Numerous similar examples demonstrate that climate change is exacerbating a whole series of current problems, to the extent of making the achievement by 2015 of the UN's Eight Millennium Objectives for Development even more illusory, though they are in fact quite modest and inadequate.[39] Beyond 2015, some specialists fear that less developed countries may fall into a spiral of under-development. Cecilia Ugaz, a Peruvian economist in charge of the UN Research Institute for Social Development, warns against the combined effects of five processes linked to global warming. These processes are a reduction in agricultural productivity; increased water shortage; extreme meteorological events; serious risks to natural eco-systems and increased health risks.[40]

The increase in population displacements for environmental reasons indicates that these fears are not without foundation. In 1999, the number of environmental refugees was for the first time higher than that of war refugees – 25 million. Since then the numbers have continued to increase.

The most important causes of population displacement are loss of soil fertility, drought, flooding and deforestation. Many of these causes are interconnected and this increases the effect on populations. Climate change is one of the interconnecting mechanisms. According to Janos Bogardi, director of the UNU–EHS: 'Especially in the poorest regions, the most significant factors in displacement are loss of soil fertility and desertification, which could be due to unsustainable soil-use interacting with climate change... Floods are another factor; these are caused by increased levels of carbon dioxide in the atmosphere, probably superimposed on natural fluctuations.'[41]

Apart from these social aspects, the specifically ecological consequences of global warming continue to give cause for concern. A glance at the Impact Chart reveals that, with a rise in temperature of about 2.5°C, a significant proportion of terrestrial ecosystems would start to emit more CO_2 than they absorb. In other words, the saturation of the carbon cycle would increase and global warming would become self-sustaining (positive retroaction).

With a rise of more than 3°C, about 30% of humid coastal zones would be lost. This is a problem, since in general these biotopes are buffers which, in the case of mangroves, mitigate the effect of exceptionally high tides, storms and cyclones.

The question of biodiversity is particularly worrying. Researchers estimate that a rise of 1°C would entail the risk of extinction for about 30% of animal and vegetable species. A rise of more than 5°C would mean the extinction of significant species in all regions of the earth. These projections are all the more alarming since other factors including soil erosion, reduction in the 'natural' or 'wilder' countryside and chemical poisoning of the atmosphere are already contributing to the danger of what biologists call 'a wave of extinction'.

Palaeontology teaches us that the biosphere has undergone five waves of extinction during its lengthy existence. The last occurred 65 million years ago when a natural disaster, without doubt a collision with an asteroid, gave rise to dust-clouds and the cooling of the climate, causing the extinction of the dinosaurs. The study of fossils in geological strata from before and after this catastrophe confirms that it gave rise to the loss of 70% of plant and animal species at a global level. Now, quite apart from the effects of global warming, the current wave of extinctions is already more significant and rapid than those that occurred so long ago.

The question of biodiversity is often not taken seriously enough in some quarters, where it is thought that one creepy-crawly more or less is not going to stop the earth in its tracks. Indeed, we can console ourselves by observing that life on earth is very inventive and probably indestructible. After every wave of extinction, diversity has started up again, more vigorously than before. Nevertheless, even if the adaptive capacities of *Homo sapiens* are infinitely superior to those of the dinosaurs, the crisis of biodiversity could cause us some serious inconveniences. Indeed apart from its significant aesthetic, affective and cultural aspects, biodiversity determines the capacity of ecosystems to adapt, especially the possibility of growing crops adapted to new conditions (drought, for example) as 90% of the human diet depends on about twenty plant cultivars.

By destroying biodiversity we are cutting off the branch we are sitting on. We are even sawing through it at both ends if, not content with having during the past century eliminated three quarters of cultivated plants, we create a warmer and drier climate in which the surviving species would be inadequate for our needs.

It is not enough, therefore, to deal with the human consequences of global warming separately from the ecological consequences. To approach it this way is simpler, but does not aid an understanding of humanity as only one part of the biosphere, dependent upon the abundance, smooth running and good health of the whole.

It would be a mistake to believe that these threats of global warming concern a hypothetical, far-off future. According to the IPCC, if our policies do not change, between now and the end of the century we can expect a rise in temperature of between 1.1°C and 6.4°C relative to 1990. The projected change means that in less than a century the earth's climate could change as much as it did during the twenty millennia that preceded it, in a way that humanity has never experienced before. 'It's not definite', is the retort from some. Agreed, not 100% definite, but it is at least 90% so. Is it reasonable to hesitate faced with a 90% - 100% probability?

Then again, it is sometimes asked, how should we react to danger when projections indicate a variation in the range of 1 to 6? It is true that the breadth of the margins of the IPCC projections is considerable. This reveals a dual uncertainty: that of climate models on the one hand, and that of the various possible scenarios for global socio-economic development on the other.[42] Confronted with such a range of possibilities people tend to put themselves into three groups; the optimists, the pessimists, and those who think it reasonable to examine both sides of the argument. The question can in fact be posed in a more rigorous way, judging by what we already know of the soundness of the IPCC estimates. Indeed, since this organisation has existed and has been creating models and projections, these models can now be compared with observable facts.

If this comparison is made we see that between 1990 and 2006 the observed increases in temperature and of those atmospheric greenhouse gases are in the higher ranges of the projection. This is already a cause for concern. But the greatest cause for concern is that the 3.3mm per annum rise in sea-level has been greater than the 2mm per annum projected by the models[43]. Some may think that a millimetre's difference is not very important but expressed as a percentage, the spread between the projection and the reality is 60% – a huge difference.

Should the increase in temperature stabilise at 2°C more than in 1780, the IPCC models project a rise in sea levels of between 0.4m and 1.4m. If we now accept the range of 60% as explained above, we obtain a possible rise of between 0.6 and 2.2m. And if we apply the saying *in medio stat virtus*[44] we arrive at a rise in sea-level of 1.4 metres – equal to the maximum in the original range...So blissful optimism is certainly not a reasonable approach, but nor is it the happy medium. In fact a certain element of pessimism, or rather of caution, is justified especially with regard to the evolution of sea levels.

What gave rise to this gap between projections and observed reality? Probably the fact that the climate models used had not perfectly and completely integrated the phenomenon of disintegrating ice caps. This weakness is no secret. The fourth IPCC report warns its readers: 'The dynamic processes linked to the melting of ice not included in current models but suggested by recent observations, could increase the vulnerability of the ice caps to warming, thus augmenting the rise in sea level in the future.'[45] But this short sentence has not received the attention it deserves. The media have been content to report that sea levels could rise from between 18 to 59 centimetres between now and the end of the century, without investigating the limits of the models. These models raise a decisive question, the difference between *the melting of ice,* a linear process, and the *disintegration of the ice caps* which is proceeding by leaps and bounds.

A parallel with the process of melting snow and avalanches will enable us to understand the question. The spring thaw causes the snow to melt drop by drop. This melting can be modelled, but the moment when melting sets off avalanches, the extent of these are subject to so many variables that projection becomes an insoluble puzzle.

Since they are not linear and are subject to so many variables, the *dynamic processes linked to the melting of ice* cannot be integrated in mathematic models, or only imperfectly. But these processes are recognised and have been observed.

During the summer months, the diurnal temperature in the Polar Regions rises slightly above zero, causing vast reservoirs of water to form on the surface of the ice caps, which create ruts in the ice. In Greenland, where the ice cap contains enough water to cause a rise in sea-level of about 6 metres, researchers have seen a 'lake' three kilometres wide empty in 90 minutes, like an ordinary wash-basin. Now, if water suddenly sinks through the crevasses of the glaciers into the rocks at the base, it could cause enormous masses of ice to break off, which would in turn cause a sharp rise in sea-level if they slipped into the ocean.

A few years ago, it was believed that these phenomena were confined to Greenland but the Antarctic has now become a major cause for concern. It should be noted that the accumulated ice mass on this continent is equivalent to a rise in sea level of 60 metres. Fortunately, the largest area (the eastern ice cap) is stable. On the other hand worrying phenomena have been observed on the peninsula, on the western ice cap and on the surrounding ice shelves.[46]

The ice accumulated on the Western Antarctica and on the peninsula – ice shelves included- is each equivalent to an increase in sea level of about five metres. On the west coast of the peninsula, the rise in temperature has no equivalent anywhere in the world – over 3°C in 50 years. In the north east, where the thermometer indicates a summer average of 2.2°C, the increase in temperature could be about 0.5 °C every ten years. The results are visible. In recent years six shelves have disintegrated, notably the huge Larsen B, a sheet of ice 220m deep and extending into the sea for 3,250 square kilometres. This 'calving' – the name given by specialists to the break between the glacier and the shelf – of Larsen B took place over a few weeks during the southern summer of 2002. It can be explained primarily by growing exposure to warm western winds caused by global warming.[47]

The danger could be even greater than in Greenland for two reasons. Firstly, the mountain valleys of the peninsula are less narrow and winding so the glaciers could slip more rapidly into the sea.[48] Indeed the speed of certain flows of ice has tripled after the calving of Larsen B. Secondly, the rocky massif supporting the western ice cap is mainly located below sea level and in several places it slopes down toward the depths of the ocean.[49] Since oceanic circulation in the Polar Regions is becoming warmer thanks to climate change, there is a danger that the submarine base of the ice cap may melt. In extreme circumstances, the combination of the melting and the 'calving' of ice caps due to water sweeping into the crevasses could result in a block 4 kilometres thick, the size of Texas, slipping into the ocean. This is the climatologists' nightmare.

For James Hansen, director of NASA's Goddard Institute for Space Studies, and for eight other high-ranking specialists who have added their signatures to his in an article in the journal *Science*, the danger is closer than might be thought.[50]

Circumventing the difficulty of modelling non-linear phenomena, Hansen and his colleagues have drawn deductions from the history of paleo-climates. It is known that the earth was almost entirely ice-free 65 million years ago, and that the glaciation of the Antarctic occurred about 35 million years ago. At this point, a qualitative threshold was passed, characterised by precise parameters in terms of solar radiation, albedo and atmospheric concentration of greenhouse gases. Once this threshold had been crossed, sea levels dropped, because precipitation at the Poles accumulated in the form of snow. Now, at the end of a close analysis, the article in *Science* has reached the conclusion that we are about to cross this threshold in a different direction.

The atmosphere is currently comprised of 385 ppm of CO_2, while the atmospheric concentration of carbon dioxide probably consisted of 350 to 500 ppm when the Antarctic ice cap was formed. According to Hansen and his colleagues, the rise in sea levels corresponding to 385 ppm would, on balance, be 'several metres at least', and the history of the earth may prove that such a rise could occur in less than a century.

Thus we may have already crossed the red line, but the slow pace of the warming of the oceans and the melting of the ice caps would grant us a reprieve of two to three decades at most in Hansen's estimation. In other words, the thermal inertia of water and ice is something the thread which held the sword above the head of Damocles. No-one can say when the thread will break, but there is no doubt that it *will* break if we continue – even for another 15 years – to increase emissions of carbon dioxide at the rate of 2 ppm a year. Indeed if we do this we will shortly reach a point of no return, after which the breaking up of the ice caps and a rise in sea levels would be inevitable and uncontrollable.

This hypothesis should be taken seriously. Hansen is not a member of the IPCC but he is the chief climatologist of NASA, and was one of the first specialists to raise the alarm on the subject of global warming. He reported to the US Congress more than 20 years ago.

Climatologist Jean-Pascal van Ypersele, vice-chair of the IPCC, says he 'fears Hansen may be right'.[51] Although subject to a certain reserve, IPCC chair Rajendra Pachauri has difficulty in concealing his concern. During a conference in Brussels in early 2009 he described the possible rise in sea levels as 'the number one danger within the framework of global warming'.[52] A few months previously he had informed the press: 'My hope is that the next IPCC report will be able to give much better information on the possible melting of the two huge ice caps (Greenland and West Antarctica) in what looks like a frightening situation'. This was just before a research visit to the Antarctic, and the IPCC president added: 'If you don't go there, you don't get a clear idea of the reality of the situation. You can read as much as you like on these subjects, but it doesn't really become part of you, you don't truly understand the size of the problem'.[53]

The size of the problem is indeed difficult to grasp – as is the urgency. If Hansen and his colleagues are right, there is simply not a moment to lose. Not only the higher range of the margins of the IPCC projections should be taken into account, but the timescale would be completely different.

The IPCC long term projections refer to a maximum rise in sea levels of 1.4m for a rise in temperature of 2°C. 'Long term' in this context means about 1,000 years, the period necessary for thermohaline mixing to homogenise the enormous masses of sea water. Now, if we hypothesise a break-up of the ice caps, a rise of 1.4 metres or more could come about before the end of the century and there would be further repercussions. Hansen and his colleagues have written that, 'if the concentration of CO_2 in the atmosphere were doubled in relation to the pre-industrial era, the final result would probably be a planet almost entirely without ice, preceded by a period of chaotic changes with continual obliteration of coastlines'.

Most of the population of the world lives in coastal plains and large deltas. These are the regions in which civilisation developed 5,000 years ago. The chaos described by Hansen would probably not mean the end of the human race but there are several reasons to fear that it would sound the death-knell of what we all recognise as 'civilisation'.

Chapter Four
A FALSE CONSCIOUSNESS

Thanks to the media we have become aware of expressions used by the IPCC such as 'anthropogenic' climate change, or warming 'due to human activity.' The Greek term *anthropos* means humanity in general and the adjective derived from it suggests a phenomenon caused by our species.

The increase in temperature we are experiencing is primarily due to the combustion of fossil fuels during the two centuries since the Industrial Revolution. The cause is therefore not 'human agency', nor humanity in general but a particular type of historically and socially determined human activity. Earlier societies are not responsible for global warming, and neither are those who continue with alternative modes of production in the present day.

Of course, to the extent that the phenomenon is not caused by a natural process, it is not entirely incorrect to claim that it is due to 'human activity'. But this is to say too much, or too little. As Bertell Ollman, professor of politics at New York University, notes in another context, 'In order to understand each specific problem, it is necessary to abstract a level of generality which reveals the characteristics which bear the greatest responsibility'.[54] Scientific analysis cannot leap from one level of logic to another. If it does, we will end up being incapable of explaining a phenomenon, and thus unable to act on it in a logical and rational manner.

It is undeniable that human beings have a particular impact on the environment, and thus also on the climate, greater than any other species in the animal kingdom. This difference is due to the fact that we produce the means of our own social existence. We draw on the resources of nature –especially energy resources – not merely to feed ourselves, but to cook our food, to make tools, and to provide clothes, housing, transport, etc. But is this 'anthropogenic' level of generality sufficient for the understanding of the damage which human societies do to eco-systems? No, because it fails to take into account another characteristic of our species that is inextricably linked to the previous characteristic. Each generation to some extent stands on the shoulders of its predecessors. Unlike social insects we do not reproduce our existence identically but develop modes of production which tend to become more and more complex. The 'anthropogenic' impact takes particular forms according to each type of society. It is these forms which are decisive in understanding the deterioration of the environment and not our characteristics as a biological species.

The link between these forms and the environment is not mechanical but dialectical. In other words, all progress of the productive forces does not necessarily lead to a degradation of the environment, an improvement is also possible. For example the agricultural revolution in Flanders in the 15th century ended the practice of leaving land fallow for three years following the discovery that leguminous plants act as a 'green fertiliser'. This lead to an increase in productivity such that there was a decrease in deforestation, and, as a consequence, soil erosion which had been significant in preceding centuries.[55] One could argue the same today. The substitution of energy from fossil fuels with that from renewable sources, the increase in energy efficiency, the development of the 'productive forces', are all necessary to save the climate and reduce atmospheric pollution. But we will argue later in the book, that this depends entirely on political and social choices.

Many writers have examined the social history of the environment.[56] But the history of the impact of climate on societies has yet to be written. It is possible that the use of fire as a primitive hunting technique may have affected water supplies and the degree of humidity in the atmosphere by damaging the plant cover in certain regions – thereby influencing local climates. Subsequently agriculture probably had a more significant impact: cultivation implies the clearing of terrain and it is known that climates are greatly affected by the presence or absence of forest cover. But we are speaking here of local climates, since population size remained limited until the 18th century. Research bears out that agriculture has had a continuous effect on climate since the Neolithic Period due to the release of carbon and the increase of surface albedo. These two mechanisms, however, operate in opposition: the first warms, the second cools. It appears difficult to establish exactly the outcome; some researchers refer to global warming on a historic time-scale[57] while others seem to favour a slight cooling...[58]

Be that as it may, there is no doubt that the extent of these impacts in the past has nothing in common with current climate change. Furthermore – and this is essential – the difference between the past and our own period is not merely quantitative but qualitative, because the underlying social dynamics are radically different:

- In hunter-gatherer or agricultural economies, environmental damage results from an endemic tendency to under-production, caused mainly by a fear of shortages. People set fire to the undergrowth to flush out the diminishing amount of game. They cut down trees during droughts so that their livestock can graze on the leaves. The period of crop-rotation in slash-and-burn cultures is reduced in order to cope with an increased hunger.
- In the contemporary world, on the other hand, the environment is endangered in the first place by the tendency towards over-production (and over consumption by those with that are better off). The major cause of environmental damage is the logic of accumulation as the incentive of competition creates an unprecedented productivism within the system. It is true that poor populations may also cause environmental damage, generally with the aim of avoiding famine, but this behaviour cannot be examined independently of the global economic context which excludes them from production and diminishes their credit-worthiness.

To speak of 'anthropogenic' climate change is to put these two different processes into the same category. It leads to the idea that the current ecological crisis is nothing more than a large-scale reproduction of previous 'anthropogenic' ecological crises. This is the a-historic view popularised by Jared Diamond in his bestseller *Collapse: How Societies Choose to Fail or Survive*,[59] in which he uses – and misuses – the metaphor of Easter Island to illustrate his thesis.[60]

In reality the ecological crisis we are currently experiencing is not part of a continuous pattern linked to those of the past but a radical new departure. No previous society has been driven by that desire for profit which leads the possessors of capital to accumulate more in order to produce more and sell more while continually creating new needs. No society in the past has developed a technology as dangerous as nuclear technology. This situation represents an unprecedented risk.

What we call the ecological crisis is more a historic crisis of the relationship between humanity and its environment. Its basic cause is over-production which leads to over-consumption on the one hand and growing poverty and under-consumption on the other. In the final analysis, therefore, it is a social crisis and it would be infinitely more accurate to refer to capitalist climate change instead of 'anthropogenic' climate change.[61]

On the first page of his lengthy report on the economics of climate change, produced at the request of the UK government, Nicholas Stern refers to 'the greatest and most widespread setback to the market that there has ever been up till now'.[62] On this point the former Chief Economist of the World Bank is closer to the truth than the experts of the IPCC but he does not investigate the question more deeply and, above all, draws no conclusion. On the contrary, in the 500 or so pages which follow, the ultra-neoliberal Stern makes a great effort to persuade us that a larger market is the only way to repair the damage caused by market excess. Can anyone understand this?

In reality, it is a bit rich to say that global warming is 'the greatest and most widespread set-back to the market'. The responsibility of the *market* for global warming is overwhelming! To be sure, the economic growth of the Industrial Revolution would not have been possible on a large scale without coal, which is the most polluting of the fossil fuels.[63]

Nevertheless, it would be a mistake to attribute climate change vaguely to 'progress', 'technology' or 'industry' in general, as does German philosopher Hans Jonas in *The Imperative of Responsibility*, for example.[64]

Firstly this is because competition has encouraged the concentration of capital which has played a role in the development of large-scale industry and consequently in the standardisation of facilities. By swallowing up smaller firms large companies have eliminated the traditional use of renewable energies such as wind and water power.

Secondly – and most significantly – competition for short-term profit very quickly ruled out the possibility of using new renewable resources which would have allowed for development while maintaining a cleaner environment and protection of human health.

In this context, it is worth digressing to discuss the vicissitudes of solar energy. Photo-voltaic solar panels have been presented as the last word in science and technology. In fact the photo-voltaic effect was discovered by the French physicist Edmond Becquerel in 1839, yet in the succeeding 130 years no organisation or government has seriously considered utilising this resource. It was not until the NASA space expeditions that anyone dreamt of exploring its potential. The contrast between the long-lasting indifference to solar production of electricity on the one hand and the immediate enthusiasm for nuclear fission on the other, is extremely striking. The development of nuclear science would not have been possible without considerable public investment, and agreed to mainly for military reasons, in spite of the terrible dangers of this technology. Research into solar energy never benefited from such support.

It will be claimed that things have started to change. This is true, but much more slowly and less significantly than is generally believed. Between 1974 and 2003, in spite of the double warning of the petrol crises of 1973 and 1979, only 2% of the research budget of countries members of the International Energy Agency was devoted to research on photo-voltaic energy (1% for thermal solar energy and 0.9% for thermo-electric solar energy).[65] Why? Because it is much cheaper to burn coal, natural gas and oil. Because the fossil fuel sector has considerable economic power that greatly influences political decision-makers. Because nuclear power (56% of research budgets) is of great interest to the military establishment and it corresponds to the Promethean fantasy of a source of energy created and controlled by humans. Because solar radiation is diffuse and the economic system has a spontaneous tendency to promote centralised and centralising mechanisms, which facilitate social control and capitalist control of the economy. Because fossil fuels, including uranium, constitute energy supplies and investors can easily take possession of deposits in order to acquire a monopoly of the resource and impose monopoly prices.

Photo-voltaic energy is far from being the only victim of this process. Its close relative, thermal solar energy, has suffered a similar fate. This case is even more striking since the technologies which would have to be implemented are very simple. There is no need for basic research on semi-conductor materials as this information has been well-known since the 18th century. Furthermore, during the second half of the 19th century, and the early 20th century, engineers in India, France, Egypt and the USA invented machines using the sun to heat and purify water, cook food, distil sea water, operate machinery, heat houses, etc.

This is the story of a technical process which could have changed the face of the world if it had been developed. When one reads the literature, it is striking to note that the inventors were looking for solutions to problems that were often identical to those of today. It is also striking to note that the technical solutions proposed were very similar to those currently presented to us as being the inventions of genius such as storage of solar heat in the earth or in water, energy-neutral houses, parabolic mirrors to concentrate solar radiation, use of hydrogen as an energy vector, fuel cells and so on.

It goes without saying that the earlier inventors were not motivated by the campaign against the increase in the greenhouse effect, since people were not yet aware of the dangers. The inventors' endeavours were nonetheless inspired by a long-term global vision which is still relevant today. John Ericsson, inventor of machines operated by steam and heat generated from solar energy, wrote: 'A few thousand years, drops in the ocean of time, will exhaust the mines of Europe if we do not have recourse to the help of the sun during this period'.

A year later, Augustin Mouchot, another inventor of solar powered machines, wrote: 'There must come a day when, in the absence of fuel, industry will be forced to return to the use of natural resources. We have no doubt that deposits of coal and oil will long continue to supply its enormous calorific power for a long time but these deposits will undoubtedly run out ... We cannot avoid the conclusion that it is wise and prudent not to be lulled into a false sense of security on this subject'.[66]

Mouchot's example deserves to be emphasised. Noted especially as the inventor of a solar-powered printing press, the teacher of mathematics at the Lycée in Tours was convinced that he held the key to the future of technology. Aware of the difficulty posed by the intermittent nature of solar radiation, he concentrated on the question of storage. He proposed to solve the problem by using solar energy to separate water into hydrogen and oxygen, then storing each element separately before re-uniting them and producing an electric current.[67] Thus a century and a half ago a free spirit had anticipated the possibility of an energy system based almost entirely on solar power, with hydrogen and electricity as vectors.[68] His dream was torpedoed by the coal industry where mass production brought economies of scale into play.

In his recent study discussing the first modern attempts to utilise solar power, Travis Bradford comments:

> This period in industrial history ushered in a grand expansion in knowledge and invention as entrepreneurs pursued many new energy technologies as alternatives to wood and coal. As in all periods of rapid technological growth, an efficient form of commercial Darwinism determined winners and losers. Inventors and entrepreneurial businessmen developed new technologies. Society adopted those that operated and performed faster, better and cheaper, while all others were put on the shelf until changing relative costs or technological breakthroughs created an economic justification to revisit them.[69]

The expression 'commercial Darwinism' suggests that the choice of technologies had been made in accordance with natural laws. In fact, this claim is more than debatable. Furthermore, Bradford contradicts himself when he gives the example of a certain Frank Shuman, an American who had designed an irrigation pump powered by steam produced by the concentration of solar power. Shuman's machine was more economical in use than all the others. The cost of its production was twice as high as that of the rival system, powered by coal, but, thanks to the fact that solar radiation is free, the initial cost could have been recovered within less than two years.

Nevertheless, coal won the day, flying in the face of all logic...

Why was research into solar power abandoned? Partly for reasons of immediate profitability, partly for other, secondary reasons such as a lack of capital on the part of the inventors; the increasing power of corporations exploiting fossil fuel; the political support they enjoyed; and the need of colonial powers to favour the technologies of the metropolis in order to offer protected markets to their industries. It goes without saying that these reasons are not the laws of nature, but of a small section of society.

Bradford writes that the choice of technologies has been efficient. This is undoubtedly the case for those owning shares in the fossil fuel industry, yet from the point of view of society as a whole *inefficiency* is the order of the day. And what inefficiency! Nicholas Stern estimates that climate change will cause damage comparable to the cumulative effects of the two World Wars and the Great Depression.[70] Disturbing as this evaluation is, it nevertheless falls short of reality because it fails to factor in the damage already caused by two centuries of fossil fuel use.

For a complete evaluation of 'efficient commercial Darwinism', it would be necessary to complete Stern's calculation by factoring in other hazards. For example silicosis – the most fatal occupational hazard of the 20th century, according to two specialists.[71] Then there is asthma – closely correlated with fine particles emitted particularly by diesel engines – and illnesses caused by lead pollution and by volatile organic compounds in petrol. Acidification of ecosystems due to emissions of sulphur oxides from power stations leads to damage while there is also the irreversible destruction of the landscape close to coal mines and oil wells, the oil spills at sea, the rise in tropospheric ozone produced by motor vehicles, and chemical poisoning of the biosphere by pesticides derived from oil.

'Efficient commercial Darwinism' only exists in the imaginations of Bradford and his followers. In fact, a series of technological alternatives have been blocked in spite of their efficiency, or even because of it, under pressure from the fossil fuel industry. This sector has inordinate power due not only to the fact that energy is indispensable for every human activity and that all investments in energy are long-term but also, and especially, due to the enormous economic power obtained by accumulating the excess profits at the expense of the rest of the economy. In 2004 Jean-Marie Chevalier, a specialist in energy markets, estimated the annual global turnover of the hydrocarbon sector at 1,500 billion euros.[72] The total cost of production amounts to a maximum of around 500 billion euros. Working on an average profit rate of 15% it can be concluded that the income or excess profit is in the region of 1,325 billion euros a year – about the equivalent of the GDP of

France. It is shared between the producing countries, the big corporations and the consuming countries by means of taxes and excise duties.[73]

With the less polluting alternatives side-lined, the negative impacts of fossil fuels have been concealed behind the 'Wall of Money'. And there is no doubt that money has delayed the recognition of the danger of climate change. Earlier, the extremely slow development of awareness was due to the uncertainty and slow nature of global warming. But since the 1980s, especially in the USA, the representatives of corporations most closely allied to fossil fuels have initiated and assiduously cultivated lobbying structures which have literally bought scientists, journalists and politicians. Their aim is to prevent the growing consensus among climatologists from reaching decision makers and public opinion.

Playing sometimes on 'science' and sometimes on scepticism towards it, sometimes on the sacrifices demanded by the Kyoto Protocol and sometimes on the insignificance of this same Protocol, these lobbies have done all in their power to relegate the reality of climate change to the category of an uncertain and controversial hypothesis. Indeed they present it as an apocalyptic religious whim, or a plot against 'The American Way of Life'.[74] Their overwhelming responsibility was denounced by top climate scientist James Hansen in an address before the US Congress worthy of someone like Naomi Klein. He told Congress:

> Special interests have blocked transition to our renewable energy future. Instead of moving heavily into renewable energies, fossil companies choose to spread doubt about global warming, as tobacco companies discredited the smoking-cancer link. Methods are sophisticated, including funding to help shape school textbook discussions of global warming. CEOs of fossil energy companies know what they are doing and are aware of long-term consequences of continued business as usual. In my opinion, these CEOs should be tried for high crimes against humanity and nature.[75]

It is difficult to avoid the conclusion that the capitalist mode of production, in its search for excess profit, is built around energy obtained from fossil fuel in spite of the damage it causes. Furthermore, this mode of production uses these resources in defiance of common sense, thus increasing their social and environmental threat. The media is full of the efforts that each of us ought to make to consume less energy such as using low-energy light bulbs, turning the thermostat down, reducing car usage, putting a lid on saucepans, etc. Although this advice is of some use, and should followed as far as possible and without moralising but it distracts our attention from the fact that the energy system is characterised by structural wastage far more significant than wastage caused by individual behaviour. The cause of this wastage is once again the pursuit of profit.

The example of the transport sector is instructive. During the 20th century the advantages of oil as a cheap and abundant source of liquid fuel with a high energy content allowed for centralised and concentrated capital to play a key role in the globalisation of transport and thus of markets, thereby occupying a strategic position in economic and political fields. From then on, in conjunction with producers of coal and electricity and large oil-dependent sectors like the automobile and aircraft industries, ship building and the petro-chemical industry, the multinational oil companies have prevented the use of alternative energy resources, technologies and distribution networks. They have encouraged over-consumption and limited the progress of energy efficiency, with regard both to systems and to products.

After the Second World War, this tendency was especially marked by the manufacture of millions of individual vehicles, huge consumers of fuel. A real triumph for the fossil fuel industry, this mass production ushered in the post-war boom. It contributed to the explosion in the use of oil – resulting in CO_2 emissions and polluting compounds – and created a widespread dependence on the car.[76]

Closer to the present day, a completely unsustainable transport system has been created. It has happened thanks to neo-liberal capitalist globalisation; the massive export of capital towards developing countries; flows of products for the global market; the maximisation of profit by transnational companies who farm out production to all four corners of the globe; the destruction of public transport systems (especially railways) and the spectacular growth in air transport and shipping.

It will take a long time to cure this dependence on the car because everything has been built up round this method of transport. But the sickness has not developed in isolation. Rather, it has been created by the corporations with the complicity of governments. The example of the United States is telling. In 1974 a report by the US Senate gave a detailed account of the way in which General Motors (GM), Standard Oil of California and the tyre manufacturer Firestone had deliberately destroyed the rail, tram and trolley-bus networks in no fewer than 45 American cities in order to extend the market for their products. This is how the report described the methods used in Los Angeles:

In 1940, GM, Standard Oil and Firestone took over active control of Pacific City Lines (the company running the electric rail lines)...that year, PCL began to acquire and eliminate the electrified sectors of Pacific, at a cost of 100 million dollars, including the rail track linking Los Angeles with Glendale, Burbank, Pasadena and San Bernadino. Subsequently, GM and Standard Oil financed a subsidiary to motorise the centre of Los Angeles. This subsidiary suppressed electric vehicles, destroyed electric transport links and tore up the rails. In short, GM and its industrial allies broke the regional rail links from Los Angeles and then motorised its city centre.[77]

In 1949 the three companies were convicted of criminal conspiracy. But justice was meted out according to the power and influence of the lobby with GM and its finance director being fined respectively 5,000 dollars and ... one dollar.[78]

The collusion between the automobile and oil industries is so close, especially in the US, that it sometimes leads to completely inappropriate investment decisions, not only from a social point of view but even from an economic point of view. For instance, in the early 1990s GM produced a high-tech electric vehicle for the Californian market, the *GM EV1*. This car was produced in different versions, entirely electric or hybrid, but was not available for sale but only on a three-year lease. The launch of this model was a response to a recently introduced law specifying that, as from 1998, 2% of cars on the road had to be 'zero emission'.

GM and other manufacturers continually contested this ruling, claiming that low energy vehicles had no economic future. The very odd bureaucratic procedures which complicated the purchase of an *EV1* were part of this strategy. Once the wording of the law had been toned down to suit the companies, the 900 or so models in use were recalled and nearly all were destroyed in spite of the protests of satisfied users. A short while later, the Detroit company launched its *Hummer* – probably the most monstrously anti-ecological vehicle in the history of the automobile – abandoning the US market to the *Toyota Prius* which became a great success.[79] It was not until 2005 that GM recognised their mistake, and hastily, but rather belatedly, tried to catch up with their Japanese competitor...

The transport system is not the only example. The electricity network constitutes another example of structural wastage. It is really absurd to centralise the production of a high-quality energy resource that is then transported long distances (causing wastage) to be utilised in situations where it would often be more rational to have recourse to a lower-quality energy resource produced on site. This criticism was expressed more than 25 years ago by the American ecologist Barry Commoner but remains entirely relevant today.[80] In the name of the second law of thermodynamics, Commoner put the case for energy efficiency to be calculated at production level, not at supply level. What is the point of building an efficient power station if the coal it burns is transported thousands of kilometres and if the electricity is used to heat water in bathrooms 200 kilometres further away?[81] It would be better to use on-site energy for this sort of thing with the assistance of solar panels or by burning local biomass.

The way of avoiding the wastage inherent in the hyper-centralisation of the network is known as 'co-generation of heat and electricity'. The principle is simplicity itself. Instead of letting the heat produced by fuels in the production of electricity dissipate into the atmosphere, it is used to heat homes and offices, or in low-energy industrial processes. The fuel saving is about 30-40% in comparison with separate production, and also entails a corresponding reduction of CO_2 emissions. Furthermore, decentralisation has a number of collateral advantages, especially the reduction of losses during transportation and the reduction of emissions detrimental to the ozone layer, caused by leakage of chlorofluorocarbon (CFC) from refrigeration units.

However, co-generation is not popular. In the EU, it represents barely 11% of electricity generation. The technology itself is in no way subversive; it is merely a rational alternative. But it involves the decentralisation of electricity production, the construction of public heat-producing networks in residential areas and inter-sector economic planning linking the producers of electricity with industrial users of moderate heat (agri-business, for example).[82]

Decentralisation, public investment, economic planning are all scare words for the energy lobbies. Careful not to annoy them, the European Commission plans to increase the proportion of co-generation from 11% - 18% during the next few years.[83] Much more ambitious targets could be adopted, as is demonstrated by the examples of Luxemburg, The Netherlands and Denmark, where usage is above 30%. Instead, people ramble on about 'anthropogenic' global warming in order to make consumers feel guilty and encourage them to buy water heaters labelled 'Energy Plus'.

The expression 'anthropogenic global warming' alone suffices to distract attention from structural mechanisms and focus on individual behaviour. In order to emerge from the ecological crisis we are told our first priority should be to stay quietly in our place in society and take personal responsibility for changing our 'lifestyle'. Businesses should produce green technologies and consumers should use them. Within this framework, there is no longer any question of modifying social relations. The campaign to stabilise the climate becomes essentially a personal matter of ethics, moderation, humility, even asceticism. Class, social inequality, capitalist lobbies and power structures disappear from the stage as if by magic, in favour of making individuals feel guilty.

The conservative religious bias of this discourse is obvious, and it is not by chance that churches have become more and more interested in the issue of climate.[84] This bias is explicit for Sir John Houghton, a former IPCC vice-president who is not only an eminent climatologist but also a fervent catholic and zealous proselytiser. Houghton has made a great contribution to the climate cause, and no-one could accuse him of ignoring the magnitude of the challenge. Nevertheless, when he was asked one day if he was an optimist or a pessimist, he replied: 'I am an optimist for three reasons; scientists the world over are working hard and collaborating, the necessary technologies are available, and God takes care of His creation'.[85]

Taken to this extreme, his optimism borders on recklessness. But this quote speaks volumes about the limited view of some scientists, religious or not, who, between their ultra-specialised domain and 'human nature' (or God, the idealised representative thereof), fail to take into account the social milieu of which they form a part, while, this 'level of generality' plays a decisive role.

What should be a real awareness? It would be humanity's capacity to understand the relationships at the heart of the social environment and the historically determined relationship of this social environment with Nature. John Houghton's optimism demonstrates that a science of climate change which ignores the responsibility of the economic system easily becomes a false consciousness of reality, that is to say the opposite of science – an ideology. But believers do not have the monopoly of this false consciousness. Indeed, if Almighty God is removed from Houghton's response, thought, which abhors a vacuum, will call upon an abstract humanism, or upon a cynical contempt for 'human nature'. It cannot be otherwise, since the key to the problem of climate change lies neither in technology nor in divine intervention, nor in appeals to goodwill and to a sense of responsibility towards future generations. It lies in the modification of social relations.

The German philosopher Max Horkheimer once said: 'Anyone who doesn't want to hear about capitalism should keep quiet about fascism'. For my part, I do not want to encourage anyone to keep quiet, let alone force them – even though this quote applies, *mutatis mutandis*, to climate change. This is why the rest of this work will discuss in detail capitalism and critiques of capitalism – Marxism, Socialism, Zero-Growth policies. Before that, however, candidates for the 'conscious production of history', as Ernst Bloch said, should examine their scientific information to verify under what conditions can the rise in temperature in the lower atmosphere be halted, and is it technically possible? This will be the subject of the next chapter.

Chapter Five
THE NECESSARY AND THE POSSIBLE

Global warming is a fact. It is too late to prevent it. The real question now is how to confine it within the maximum possible limits and organise the transition to an economy without fossil fuel. Meanwhile society will have to adjust to the inevitable results of its effects. In the jargon of climate negotiation, the two aspects of the question are described respectively as *mitigation* and *adaptation*. The latter is generally under-estimated by commentators, although for the people of the South – most of the human race – it is a major challenge to be dealt with urgently. The full extent of this challenge will be clearer once we have taken the measure of the constraints to be observed in order to stabilise the climate at the least dangerous level, examined the possibilities of facing up to them and assessed government policies by this criterion. These questions will form the subject of this and the following chapters.

We will begin with the physical constraints. The starting point of the argument is that greenhouse gases have a certain lifespan in the atmosphere; 100 years for CO_2, a dozen years for methane, 120 years for nitrous oxide, many thousands of years for certain industrial gases.[86] It is therefore not sufficient to stabilise emissions in order to stabilise the atmosphere; they have to be quickly and radically reduced in order to meet stabilisation targets.

The 2007 IPCC report proposes six scenarios of stabilisation, corresponding to as many possible levels of concentration of greenhouse gas in the atmosphere. Chart I indicates: a) the corresponding projections for each level in terms of average surface temperature increase and rise in sea level; b) the reductions in emissions to be achieved between now and 2050; c) the final moment at which these reductions must be implemented at a global level in order to meet the target.[87] The most radical of these six scenarios would allow for a limit in average temperature increase of $2°C$ to $2.4°C$ compared to the pre-industrial period. As temperatures have already risen by $0.7°C$ since 1780, this would mean that they could rise to a maximum of 1.3°C to 1.7°C by the end of the 21st century.[88]

Incidentally, it is astonishing to note that the media continue to report climate negotiations as if the major concern were not to let the temperature rise above 2°C. In fact this limit can probably no longer be achieved and specialists have in any case revised their estimates downwards, currently placing the threshold of danger at 1.5°C. Furthermore, the President of the IPCC publicly expressed his astonishment that the EU, which had made the 2°C figure the target of its climate policies in 1996, had not subsequently revised the figure downwards, based on new specialist reports.[89]

We have seen that the higher the temperature, the higher the social and environmental cost. The casual way in which some people resign themselves to this viewpoint is incredible. For instance *The Economist* magazine wrote that we are moving towards a set of measures corresponding to a reasonably safe rise in temperature of between 2.8°C and 3.2°C.[90] The highly neo-liberal weekly has a peculiar conception of what reasonably safe means. According to the IPCC chart, global warming on this scale would have very serious consequences, especially in terms of agricultural production and human health ('severe consequences for health systems'). If we consider in addition the danger of ice breaking up, there can be no question of opting at the very least for the IPCC's most radical scenario, meeting the conditions for its implementation and hoping that it will subsequently be possible to bring the rise in temperature to below 2°C.

So what are these conditions? According to the experts, it is a question of stabilising the atmospheric concentration of carbon dioxide at between 350 to 400ppm CO_2. The current rate stands at 385ppm CO_2 and the annual increase is about 2ppm. This confirms there is almost no room for manoeuvre. The result is the same if all greenhouse gases are taken into account.[91] In this case, the threshold that must not be crossed is between 445ppm and 490ppm of CO_2 equivalents (CO_2 eq), and here too we have already reached the danger point.

According to the IPCC, to remain below the limit of 350ppm to 400ppm of CO_2 (or 445ppm to 490ppm CO_2 eq) requires a decrease in world emissions to begin by 2015 at the latest. The decrease would then have to continue steadily in order to reach zero, or even to become negative[92], by the end of the century via a global reduction of between 50% - 80% by 2050 (Chart I).

The importance of this data cannot be over-emphasised, nor can the necessity of using it when discussing publications and statements on climate. It is important to be vigilant and ensure that those who claim to rely on the IPCC have understood the figures correctly. This is not generally the case with politicians. However, there are numerous inaccuracies even in works considered serious and reputable. Pressure from the lobbies obviously contributes to this, but it is also as though there is a sort of self-censorship, a burying of heads in the sand that prevents people from seeing 'the size of the problem' described by Rajendra Pachauri.[93]

Chart I
Classification of scenarios according to different targets of stabilisation

Category	Atmospheric concentration of CO_2 (1)	Atmospheric concentration of all greenhouse gases (2)	Average global rise in temperature in comparison with the pre-industrial period	Year of peak emissions	Change in global emissions by 2050 (in comparison with 2000)
I	350-400	445-490	2.0-2.4°C	2000-2015	-85% to -50%
II	400-440	490-535	2.4-2.8°C	2000-2020	-60% to -30%
III	440-485	535-590	2.8-3.2°C	2010-2030	-30% to +5%

According to IPCC 2007. Contribution of Working Group III to the 2007 report, Technical Summary, Chart TS.2 page 39 (Scenarios IV to VI, with no reduction of emissions in comparison with 2000 are not reproduced here; this would indicate rises in temperature of between 3.2°C and 6.1°C). (1) in ppm CO_2. (2) in ppm CO_2 eq.

Not only is this physical constraint drastic but it is linked to socio-political constraints that are no less drastic. In effect, the reductions of 50% - 80% mentioned above constitute global targets. So how is the responsibility to be distributed when we know that most of current global warming is due to the economic activities of developed countries which have been burning fossil fuels for two centuries? Obviously, it is not easy to determine the historical responsibility of each country for all gases and all activities. But we do have reliable estimates for the energy sector and for cement works. For these highly polluting sectors we can go quite a long way back into the past, relying on business and state archives. These sources supply information on the quantity of fuel used, from which the quantities of CO_2 released by combustion can be deduced. On this basis specialists consider that 70% - 80% of climate change can be attributed to developed countries.

This statistic may seem incompatible with some information in the press: the media keep informing us that China has overtaken the US as the major producer of greenhouse gases. As an absolute figure, calculated on an annual basis, this is correct. But this information evades the issue in three ways.

Firstly, it refers to the current situation, without looking at historical responsibilities. Secondly, it fails to take the population factor into account. For instance one human being in five is Chinese and a single citizen of China produces 5.5 tonnes of CO_2 a year, while a single American produces 23.5.[94] Thirdly, it does not take into account the fact that Western businesses carry out part of their production in countries with low wages – where the corresponding emissions are evaluated – but sell their goods in developed countries.

The case of China, that workshop of the world, is eloquent. A third of emissions from this country – almost as much as the combined outputs of France, Germany and the UK – results from the production of goods for export, most of which are destined for developed countries.[95] For Beijing, these emissions which are known as 'grey emissions' ought to be added to the emissions from Western countries where the goods are consumed and classified as 'domestic' emissions .[96] Such an adjustment would show a drop in Chinese emissions to 3.1 tonnes per person per annum. Those of the US, on the other hand, would increase to 29 tonnes.[97] In many developed countries, adding 'grey' emissions to 'domestic' emissions would mean that the latter would be almost doubled. On the face of it, Switzerland is a clean country, but on this basis, it would see its annual emissions of CO_2 rise from 5.8 tonnes to more than 10 tonnes.[98]

In short, it is not sufficient to say that discharges must be reduced by 50% - 80% on a global scale by 2050. The campaign against the climate tipping point concerns the whole world but justice and common sense require everyone's responsibilities to be taken into account, everyone's capacity for action, everyone's financial and technical resources etc. Although of a different nature from physical constraints, this demand for climate justice is unavoidable. A global agreement to save the climate can only be envisaged on this basis. Furthermore, the UNFCCC[99] (Rio, 1992) has been obliged to put it into practice by adopting the principle of 'common but differentiated responsibilities' for rich and poor countries.[100]

The fourth evaluative report of the IPCC thus proposes, for different levels of stabilisation, a distribution chart for efforts to reduce emissions for different groups of countries (Chart II).[101] That chart is much more important – but much less well known – than the one showing the goal of reduction on a global scale of between 50% - 85% (in which the figure of 85% is often omitted!). Two main conclusions emerge from this: 1) the situation is so serious that no plan for stabilisation worthy of the name is possible without some effort by developing countries, even the poorest, 2) the effort to be made by developed countries is quite simply Herculean.

The last line of the chart constitutes a sort of demonstration *ad absurdum*. It shows that to exempt Less Developed Countries from any limitation on emissions would not be possible except by aiming at a stabilisation of 650 ppm CO_2eq. In this case, Africa would not need to take any measures before 2050, whilst the other regions of the South could wait until 2020 before starting to act. But this is an unacceptable choice, primarily because it would involve a rise in temperature of between 3.2°C and 4°C (in comparison with the pre-industrial era) with consequences even more dangerous than those designated as 'minor' by *The Economist*. The rise in sea level, for instance, would be to between 60 cm and 2.4 metres (without taking into account the risk of glacier break-up). Poor countries would thus have to cope with damage far outweighing the advantages gained from continuing to burn fossil fuels for a few years as though nothing were happening.

On the other hand, the first line of the chart corresponds to the most radical scenario of stabilisation at a global level – which would allow for a rise in temperature not much above 2°C. It demonstrates that, in order to participate, developed countries would need to reduce their emissions by 80% - 95% between now and 2050, via an intermediate stage of reduction of 25% - 40% before 2020. In this plan – the only reasonable one – the contribution of the Global South would be far from negligible.

Africa would be able to wait until 2020 before taking action, but other 'developing' regions would have to ensure a 'substantial reduction' (between 15% - 30%) of their emissions in comparison with the forecast. It is a question of a relative reduction, less drastic than the reduction in developed countries, which is absolutely necessary. Other things being equal, it could be achieved by halting deforestation and implementing a series of simple measures in the matter of energy efficiency. But a scenario where 'all other things are equal' is not acceptable for the Global South which obviously cannot resign itself to underdevelopment.

Chart II
Range of deviations between emissions in 1990 and target emissions from 2020-2050 for various levels of concentration for developed countries and developing countries according to groups

Category	Groups of countries	2020	2050
A - 450 ppm CO_2 eq	Developed countries	-25% to -40%	-80% to -95%
	Developing countries	Substantial deviation in relation to scenario for Latin America, the Middle East, Eastern and Central Asia	Substantial deviation in relation to scenario with reference to all regions
B - 550 ppm CO_2 eq	Developed countries	-10% to -30%	-40% to -90%
	Developing countries	Deviation in relation to scenario for Latin America, the Middle East and East Asia	Deviation in relation to scenario for most regions, especially Latin America and the Middle East
C - 650 ppm CO_2 eq	Developed countries	0% to -25%	-30% to -80%
	Developing countries	No deviation	Deviation in relation to the scenario for Latin America, the Middle East and East Asia

IPCC 2007 : Contribution of Working Group III, page 776. Scenarios A, B and C correspond approximately to scenarios I, III and IV of Chart 1.

It is unacceptable that there are a billion people without access to electricity, at least 900 million without clean drinking water and more than a billion who are victims of chronic famine. Building hospitals, schools, railways, homes, power stations, water purification plants, etc., all requires significant energy resources. If these resources were to be derived from fossil fuels, the planet could not sustain it. What is the conclusion? The fundamental and inalienable right to development cannot be realised unless the South bypasses the 'fossil stage' that the developed countries have gone through, that is to say unless its development is based on the most efficient, renewable technologies. This also implies a different type of development, discussed later in this book. Meanwhile, since developing countries have no access to the necessary tools, a massive transfer of appropriate technology is needed.[102]

The conditions for saving the planet may thus be summarised as follows, taking into account both the physical constraints and the principle of 'common but differentiated responsibilities':

- Developed countries must reduce their emissions by between 25% - 40% between now and 2020, and by between 80-95% by 2050, in relation to 1990 levels;
- The level of emissions for developing countries must be reduced by 15% - 30% in relation to the plan envisaged for all regions by 2050, and almost everywhere (except Africa) by 2020;
- Global emissions must reach their highest point by 2015 and must be reduced by 50% - 85% by 2050, in comparison with levels in 2000;
- The transfer of appropriate technologies must enable the peoples of the Global South to develop their economies without causing the climate to deteriorate.

It must be emphasised that this quartet of targets is a bare minimum, for two reasons. Firstly, this will only just allow the rise in temperature to be maintained between 2°C and 2.4°C, in comparison with the 1780 level, whilst the danger threshold is in fact in the region of 1.5°C. Secondly, the impacts have been underestimated because of the difficulty of modelling non-linear phenomena.[103] In cases of doubt, the basic requirement should be to align with the IPCC's most drastic targets for reduction, considering them as a minimum. This would mean a reduction in global emissions of at least 85% by 2050, which for developed countries would require a reduction of 40% by 2020 and of 95% by 2050. Anything else would be a flagrant contradiction of the precautionary principle.

Is this technically feasible? The more time elapses, the more difficult it is to reply in the affirmative. In broad terms, the question breaks down into two parts, corresponding to the two principle causes of global warming. 1) Is it possible to put an end to deforestation? 2) Is it possible to do without fossil fuels?

As to the first question, it is perfectly possible to halt the devastation of the forests since land that has already been cleared is sufficient to meet human needs. Moreover, it must be emphasised that a correct identification of the causes of deforestation is particularly important. The destruction of forests is often blamed on indigenous peoples who practice slash-and-burn agriculture, which results in the stigmatisation of communities whose historical responsibility for global warming is negligible. Certainly it cannot be denied that in some cases poverty leads people to plunder their resources, but it is also important to investigate the underlying reasons. Researchers who have investigated the topic have concluded that the main causes of deforestation are the thirst for profit and corruption among local officials.[104] Therefore, instead of the finger being pointed at the most impoverished communities and at indigenous peoples, the priority should be to combat productivist logic and the enormous waste of forestry resources it causes.[105]

The second question about fossil fuels is by far the most important considering the development of different sources of greenhouse gases over the past three decades. What emerges is that not only are fossil fuels the principal source, but also that the amount of fossil CO_2 in global emissions is obviously increasing more rapidly than that of greenhouse gases from other sources, the contributions of which remain relatively stable.[106]

Doing without fossil fuels therefore constitutes *the* major challenge of the campaign against global warming for various, overlapping reasons. Coal and natural gas serve 80% of the energy needs of the planet. Energy installations such as power stations with a life-span of 30 or 40 years are infrastructures that cannot be changed overnight. Oil, the most popular of fossil fuels, plays a decisive role in transport, without which the global economy could not function. Lastly, 'black gold' is not only a fuel but also the basic material of the petro-chemical industry which makes pesticides, synthetic textiles, plastics, cosmetics etc. While pesticides poison the biosphere, the other petro-chemical products end up in incinerators which discharge their carbon content into the atmosphere in the form of CO_2.

Nevertheless, complicated does not mean impossible to resolve. Theoretically, it should be possible to do away completely with fossil fuels without having recourse to nuclear energy or returning to living in caves. How? By using the sun as a principal energy source. This claim still meets with a sarcastic response from many engineers who forget that fossil fuels are nothing but a reserve of solar energy transformed into biomass and then fossilised. Rather than raiding the stores it is *a priori* more intelligent to utilise the source. It does not pollute, is available in abundance throughout the surface of the earth, and is inexhaustible on a human time-scale.[107]

Currently available deposits of oil, gas and coal constitute a stockpile of energy amounting to 47,800 exajoules (EJ).[108] About 15,000 EJ existing in the form of tar sands and oil shale can be added to this bringing the total amount to around 62,000 EJ.[109] The energy content of these reserves which have taken hundreds of millions of years to accumulate is more than 40 times lower than the solar energy which reaches the surface of the earth in a single year. Nevertheless, it would be more useful to compare our needs with the supply of solar energy. In 2005, the global economy consumed 11 gigatonnes of oil-equivalent primary energy, the equivalent of 458 EJ. This is 6,000 times less than the solar flux that reached the earth during the same period.

The great advantage of fossil fuels is that they are concentrated. But the diffuse energy of the sun can also be concentrated, and nature takes care of this, not only by fossilisation but also in other, speedier ways. Marine currents, biomass, wind, waves and hydraulic power are nothing but solar energy transformed and concentrated.[110] This concentration is less than that of oil, coal and gas, but solar energy can also be artificially concentrated, thanks to parabolic reflectors, in a process of solar thermo-dynamics. It has been known since Lavoisier's time that this method allows the production of temperatures hot enough to melt metals.[111]

The intermittent nature of sunlight is also not an insuperable obstacle. In this case, the solution proposed by Augustin Mouchot is still relevant. It involves using solar energy to separate hydrogen and oxygen in water by hydrolysis, storing the elements and then re-combining them in fuel cells in order to produce electricity on demand. Other simple and well-known techniques could complete the system such as heat pumps using solar energy stored in the ground or in water; solar pumps working during the day to bring river water into reservoirs; solar radiation being used to power flywheels, whose energy could be recovered by braking, or compressed air.

The world supply of primary energy in 2008 was 492 EJ. But according to a recent report from the IPCC on renewable, the possible solar energy available could be between 1,575 and 49,837 EJ a year.[112]

The enormous potential of renewables can obviously not be placed entirely at the service of human needs. The concept to be considered is the technical potential, that is to say, the fraction of the theoretical potential usable with the technologies available at any given moment. Estimates of this potential vary enormously, but are in any case much higher (six to 18 times) than the quantity of energy consumed annually throughout the world.[113] The size of the range may give rise to scepticism but it is essentially due to larger uncertainties concerned with the possibilities of exploiting geo-thermal energy and above all energy from the seas. If these two sources are excluded, the range narrows. The author supports the argument that the cumulative potential of energy from solar, thermal, photovoltaic and thermodynamic sources, and from wind, biomass and hydraulic power, could cover five or six times the global need for primary energy.

Furthermore, the enormous gap between the theoretical and the technical potential allows us to maintain that the technical potential can be considerably increased, given the means.

This hope is confirmed in particular by developments in the photovoltaic field. As we have seen, the ability of semi-conductors to produce electricity was of no interest to governments until 130 years after its discovery, when NASA engineers were looking for an energy source for their space capsules. At that time the rate of conversion of sunlight into electricity was less than 5%. Today it is more than 18% for first generation photovoltaic cells (silicon), in spite of the relative modesty of research budgets.

It is agreed that much greater progress is still possible in the field of second-generation (multi-layered) cells. Especially those of the third generation based on technology known as 'quantum dots' would double, or indeed triple, the rate of conversion (a theoretical rate of more than 60%). Furthermore, progress is expected not only in the field of silicon-based cells, but also in organic cells which are promising because the ecological impact of making them will doubtless be minimal. Progress could be very rapid if the development of renewable energy sources could be made an absolute political priority.

Literature on renewables shows the scale of what could be achieved within a very short space of time, with very well known systems, if investment in energy were no longer subordinated to the imperatives of private profit. This book does not have the space to go into all the examples but there is enormous energy in the oceans, in particular, if this were converted into electricity using sea-turbines (a sort of submarine wind-turbine) and special buoys.

The potential marine energy off the coast of Scotland (waves, currents and tides) estimated at almost 80 TWh per annum, would suffice to supply the electricity needs of the entire region.[114] In tropical waters the difference in temperature between the warm surface waters and deeper waters would enable the production of electricity according to the principle of the heat pump, but on a very large scale. It is called the system of OTEC (Ocean Thermal Energy Conversion) which would allow the production of all the electricity for an island such as Hawaii.[115]

Another example too rarely mentioned is that of mini and micro-hydraulic power stations, installations not fundamentally different from the water mills of the past which capitalism eliminated in the course of its development.[116] The global technical potential of these small generators of electricity is not precisely known because the interest for the market remains relatively marginal. The IPCC suggests a figure of between 150,000 and 250,000 MW.[117] Certain estimates by country are more precise. The Department of the Environment for the Philippines, for instance, estimates the potential for the archipelago at about 1,300 MW, of which less than 90 MW are exploited.[118]

Nevertheless, when all is said and done, the interest in these examples is very limited and it must be clearly stated that the solution does not basically lie in technical development but in the political will to do everything possible to avoid reaching the climate tipping-point, however much it costs.

This primacy of politics is very well expressed by physicist Robert Socolow known for his work on energy transition who says:

'I am repeatedly asked what I can say about the feasibility of this or that project. I really think that is not the right question. Let us think about comparable problems we have confronted in the past, which, like this one, seemed so difficult that it was hardly worth seeking a solution. Take child labour, for instance. We decided that we would no longer accept it ... Slavery also presented similar problems ... then something clicked; everyone recognised that it could not be tolerated ... Of course this decision had a social cost. I suppose it increased the price of cotton. But we recognised that, from the moment we decided to put an end to this system of exploitation that was the price to pay.'[119]

Ironically, Robert Socolow is Vice-President of the Carbon Mitigation Initiative, founded and financed by the oil company BP. We can bet that he had no subversive intentions when he expressed this opinion. Furthermore, we can detect a subtext, a plea for everyone, rich or poor, to tighten their belts. But the parallel with the abolition of slavery or child labour is very relevant as discussions of economic feasibility are in effect expressions of 'intolerable' determination to save a 'system of exploitation' which we can perfectly well 'put an end to'. Thus, independent of the will of its author, this quote enables us to enter into a political discussion of modes of production, consumption and the alternatives.

Chapter Six
THE DOUBLE OBSTACLE POSED BY CAPITALISM

Houghton is right – 'the technologies are there'. So is Socolow, we can decide to put an end to the 'system of exploitation', which is the cause of our concerns; it is a question of political choice. But let us beware of simplistic conclusions. We will not escape from the climate trap simply by liberating green technologies from 'the constraints of the capitalist race for profit', to paraphrase Marx. The situation so very serious that we urgently need to reduce energy consumption and the production and transport of materials at the same time. The system presents us with not one but two major obstacles: the race for profit and the growth of material production (which inevitably implies the growth of consumption). Although these are linked by the same logic of competition inherent in capitalism, it will be useful in the first instance to analyse them separately. This approach will enable us to avoid a stereotypical discourse and to emphasise the unprecedented nature and the extreme seriousness of the situation. To save the climate on a global scale, we need to produce less and production needs to be located closer to consumers.

Let us start with the simpler of the two obstacles, the race for profit. Renewable energy sources are without exception more expensive than fossil fuels and will remain so for some time. Neo-liberal economists, unaware of the technological potential, have developed their perspective from two other concepts: market potential and commercial potential. The first is the amount of technological potential which can be exploited under market conditions. I will just quote this for the record, as no responsible politician believes any longer that it is possible to save the climate by the spontaneous interplay of competition and 'progress'. The key idea is that of commercial potential. An unsuitable term, which implies a political will to direct the market. The idea is to promote renewables by setting a price for carbon which would include the cost of damage caused by global warming (known as 'externalities' by economists), and which would more fully take into account the needs of future generations.[120] The problem then is to work out what to include and how to evaluate in monetary terms the disappearance of a species of butterfly, of a landscape or even of several thousands of people without resources. This problem becomes acute when the effects are delayed, because how can the costs of damage which will become evident in 20 years time be evaluated? This means that commercial potential varies considerably according to choices which, in the final analysis, are political. In his conclusion to a summary of the theoretical debates on this subject, the British economist Simon Kyte has the intellectual honesty to admit that

> The uncertainties around climate change and the long time horizons involved in economic assessment of its impacts mean that it is currently next to impossible to come to a purely 'economic' decision as to how much mitigation action should be undertaken.[121]

The fact that governmental climate strategies are essentially guided by different varieties of commercial potential reveals a choice with strong ethical implications. In the final analysis, what is the significance of the three indicators? It is very simple; basing one's arguments on technological potential amounts to saying that one is committed to stabilising the climate to the maximum extent that is still possible, mobilising all known means, whatever the cost. Adopting one of the other concepts means trying to stabilise the climate as long as it costs nothing (market potential) or not too much (commercial potential), and as long it allows businesses to make profits.

The choice of commercial potential is shocking, and reveals the true face of capitalism; not only that, it takes liberties with logic. In fact, this is a recurrence of the problem of 'levels of generality', the level corresponding to the physical problem of climate stabilisation is, according to all the evidence, that of technological potential. Being guided by commercial potential would mean placing capitalist profitability at the heart of the debate: as if the figures of NASDAQ[122] or CAC40[123] were subject to the same natural laws as the radiative power of CO_2.

A small example will show how this sleight-of-hand can obscure the perception of what is possible. A group of experts presented to the European Commission a report estimating that EU electricity needs could be met in their entirety by placing photovoltaic panels on all south-facing roofs within the EU.[124] The website of the French National Institute for Solar Energy refers briefly to this information, then adds, in response to the evidence, 'There is therefore an enormous potential, even if it is inconceivable to cover every roof with solar panels'.[125] But why is it inconceivable? Is it because, as there are not enough people able or rich enough to make the investment, a public body would have to make the necessary investments for the good of the community? or because capitalism could not allow such a vital domain as the supply of electricity to escape from the profit motive?

Nevertheless, let us leave ethics and logic to one side. Given the urgency of the situation, let us accept for a moment the necessity for pragmatism and examine the key question; can climate constraints be respected by following a political path based on commercial potential rather than technological potential – that is to say, by fixing a carbon price according to deterioration caused by global warming? First of all, at what level should the price of carbon be fixed for commercial potential to be significant?

Expressed in US dollars, the cost of electricity distributed to urban zones varies between 2 to 3 cents per KW hour.[126] The cost of renewables remains considerably greater for most technologies – 8 – 20 cents per KWh for marine energy, 12 – 18 cents per KWh for thermo-dynamic solar energy, 25 -125 cents per KWh for photovoltaic solar energy, 5 – 15 cents per KWh for biomass power stations, 5 – 13 cents per KWh for wind turbines – only large scale hydraulic and geothermal power can, under certain conditions, compete on price with fossil fuels.[127] Solar energy is also well placed but, for the other technologies the road towards capitalist profitability is a long one. Too long, in any case to hope that this approach will meet the deadlines fixed by the IPCC for 2015, 2020 and 2050.

The economists of Working Group III of the IPCC compiled 'bottom up'[128] studies with the aim of estimating, sector by sector, the commercial potential of reduction of emissions which could be achieved for less than 100 dollars per tonne of CO_2.[129] The result is disappointing, at this price, it would hardly be possible to stabilise in 2030 the amount of CO_2 released into the atmosphere at the levels that prevailed in 2000. This is very far from the reduction of 25 – 40% by 2020 (in relation to 1990) proposed by the IPCC, and much further from the minimum of 40% dictated by prudence. At a rough estimate, it would be necessary to increase the cost of carbon at least fivefold in order to remain within the limits of 2°C – 2.4°C. This is confirmed by the International Energy Agency. In order to reduce emissions to 50% between now and 2050 – which, it reminds us, is probably not enough – it estimates that it would be necessary to fix a marginal price for CO_2 of between 500 and 700 dollars a tonne in the transport sector.[130] However, this type of proposition is largely speculative. In fact – and this is the crux of the matter – there is no guarantee that flexibility between emissions and the price of carbon would be enough on its own to achieve the targets set by the IPCC.

Why? Social reactions form one unknown factor. Business leaders are already complaining loudly at the prospect of having to pay out 100 dollars for every tonne of CO_2 above a certain level of emission. Let us suppose for a moment – a hypothesis from political fiction – that a strong global power were able to impose an overall price for CO2 related to climate constraints. It is obvious that then the large corporations would pass the cost on to the end-users. In the knowledge that the burning of a tonne of diesel fuel emits 2.7 tonnes of CO_2, everyone can do their own calculations and conclude that setting a price (or levying a tax) of 500 dollars per tonne would abruptly diminish the disposable income of the majority of the population to a very significant degree.[131] The impact would be particularly great for certain categories of small businesses (farmers, fishermen, haulage contractors) whose economic activity is closely linked to oil, and whose protest movements are able to paralyse, or at least slow down, environmental politics, as they have a direct effect on the administrative decisions of neo-liberalism. As for the general population, there was a justified outcry in France in 2009, provoked by the plan for a carbon tax of 30 euros per tonne, later reduced to 17 euros, and then invalidated by the Constitutional Council.[132] This was a good example of the difficulties of a policy which, by gambling on the price of fossil fuels without previously creating conditions for reducing their use, and by increasing exemptions for businesses, shows its true nature – it is another transfer of wealth to large capitalist undertakings.

Here we approach the nub of the insoluble contradictions debated by the theoreticians of 'internalisation of externalities'. On the one hand, environmental efficiency would require the rapid implementation of a very high price for carbon, so as to promote the commercial potential of renewables above fossil fuels, but on the other hand every price increase is regarded as an attack on the competitiveness of businesses ... which mainly use fossil fuels. Of course, with fine capitalist logic, the cost could be transferred to the working people, but for that it would be necessary to crush any social resistance. Even in this case, businesses would soon be in trouble, because stifling the demand would mean stifling the economy. In short, wherever we look, there is nothing but stumbling blocks for the decision makers, who – playing it by ear – effectively determine commercial potential according to the relationship between social and economic forces. The practical result is that projects for reduction of emissions driven by a price for carbon are at one and the same time unacceptable from a social point of view and totally inadequate from an ecological point of view and it is not possible to see how it could be otherwise.

The Stern report, for instance, argues the case for carbon to have a single global price, to be added to the price of goods and services. No precise amount is suggested, but this proposal is a flagrant injustice. In developing countries, the transfer to goods and services of a global price for carbon determined by the cost of environmental damage caused by industries in the North would mean in effect that less developed countries would end up paying the full amount of the bill, in relation to their purchases. The principle of common but differentiated responsibilities is reversed. Stern suggests that in developing countries the revenue of a carbon tax (or the product of the sale of emission quotas – this is not important) should be paid into social security in order to compensate for a drop in employers' pension contributions which, Stern says, would become necessary due to competition from countries with low wages. But it is an obvious trap, if the tax is ecologically effective, social security revenues will drop, and the question then arises – where do we find the funds to make up the deficit?

The key point to be emphasised here is that the environmental inefficiency of this proposal is equal to its social injustice. The ex-chief economist of the World Bank is in effect proposing a carbon price aimed at stabilising the concentration of greenhouse gases at between 500 to 550 ppm CO_2 eq. This is clearly more than the 445 – 490 ppm CO_2 eq proposed by the IPCC as the threshold to keep within the limit of a 2°C rise in temperature, but Stern claims that it can be done in no other way without plunging the economy into profound crisis. Thus, having pretended to share the concerns of the scientists, having put the case for acting urgently, the author changes his tone abruptly; he writes:

> The lesson here is to avoid doing too much, too fast, and to pace the flow of mitigation appropriately. For example, great uncertainty remains as to the costs of very deep reductions. Digging down to emissions reductions of 60-80% or more relative to baseline will require progress in reducing emissions from industrial processes, aviation, and a number of areas where it is presently hard to envisage cost-effective approaches.[133]

We see here how those in power, well aware of the risks, nevertheless arrive at completely irresponsible conclusions, which gives their discourse a schizophrenic character.

What are these costs, then? Stern estimates that his plan would cost 1% of GDP, as opposed to 3% for a stabilisation at the most radical level proposed by the IPCC. Considering that global GDP represents about 6,000 billion dollars, the bill for the IPCC's most drastic scenario would be in the region of 1,800 billion dollars. From one point of view, this is a small amount. By way of comparison, global military expenditure in 2004 amounted to 1037 billion dollars (the USA was responsible for 47% of this)[134], and, as we have seen, the hydrocarbon sector rakes in excess profits of about 1,300 billion euros per annum. But from the point of view of the shareholders of the above-mentioned sectors, it is far too much. Now, these sectors occupy a dominant position in contemporary capitalism. To conclude, in the short period of 40 years which is left to us, one cannot envisage how the system could instigate a transition in energy use at the necessary or possible level with its mechanisms of price, competition and the market.

We decided to analyse separately the two obstacles on the road to an optimum stabilisation of the climate: the race for profit and the logic of accumulation. We turn now to the second. The situation may be summarised as follows: renewables cannot replace fossil fuels unless energy consumption is radically reduced in the most developed capitalist countries, and the size of this reduction is such that it necessitates in turn a certain reduction in the production and transport of materials.

In order to grasp this point, it must be understood that transition does not consist merely of replacing one energy source by another, like changing fuel at the pump. On the contrary, it involves completely replacing one energy *system* by another, the characteristics of which will be very different, because of the different sources.[135] Solar energy is diffuse and usable in different forms, which are not all available in all regions, and require the use of specific converters (wind turbines, sea turbines, solar thermal panels, photovoltaic panels, different forms of biomass converters, parabolic mirror systems, etc). A centralised energy system would therefore have to give way to a system that was centrally coordinated but very decentralised. Furthermore, in order to resolve the problem of energy storage, it would be necessary to have recourse to a new vector – hydrogen, the production and distribution of which requires special equipment. In a word, while the current system is governed by the partial logic of cost-effectiveness, calculated installation by installation in a context of competition, its successor will have to favour global thermodynamic efficiency, which will mean planning independently of costs, in a context of cooperation. *Last but not least,*[136] the global approach will have to include agriculture, because green plants, in their capacity as natural converters of solar energy, are an integral part of the energy system. As a concrete example, even if it is profitable from a capitalist viewpoint, it is absurd to expend more energy on producing fertilisers than the biomass grown with these fertilisers will produce when it is burnt.

At some point the scale of the theoretical potential of renewables and the enormous gap between the current technical potential may allow us to think that a system of solar energy, once installed, would open considerable possibilities for qualitative – indeed, quantitative – human development. Our proposal is not, therefore, to reject the very idea of progress. The problem is that this long-term hope does not allow us to leapfrog over the problems of short and medium term transition. Now, this transition, apart from the fact that it needs to be achieved within 40 years, involves structural upheavals, including not only decentralisation, restructuring and the cessation of some activities, but also considerable investment in new infrastructures.

Use of photovoltaic potential will allow us to understand the difficulty. It has already been indicated that installing photovoltaic panels on all south-facing roofs in the EU would generate all Europe's electricity needs. However, from the point of view of global energy efficiency, it would be absurd to install solar panels in buildings that have not previously been insulated. Currently, 60% of EU housing stock is still fitted with ordinary glass windows and, as a rule, houses in most countries are thermal sieves, with no insulation in floors, attics or walls. So it is not only a question of making millions of solar panels, but also of large quantities of insulation, of repairing roofs, adapting houses, building new ones, etc.

It is clear that all this requires a significant public investment plan, without which the potential for reducing emissions will be seriously limited by the imperative to make a profit. This is obvious in the housing sector. While buildings represent about one-third of CO_2 emissions, the targets of the commission, formulated in the Directive on energy emissions from buildings, do not exceed an increase in efficiency of 1% per annum. Why? Because neo-liberal orthodoxy blocks recourse to publicly funded initiatives, which could achieve a greater energy efficiency by providing what is necessary to those unable to afford them.[137] The same logic applies in other fields; massive investments are required in order for public transport to replace individual cars, and for railways and waterways to replace lorries. A decentralised network of installations using renewables, with co-generation and heat distribution networks, must replace the current hyper-centralised network, a whole infrastructure must be established to allow the use of hydrogen produced from renewable sources. A public policy of restructuring of town and country planning is imperative, aimed at fighting urban sprawl and the increase of industrial estates in the middle of the countryside, etc.

Up to this point, the Left is in its element; developing the public sector. The snag is that these investments call for material production ... thus an energy source which, at least in the first phase of transition, must be mostly fossil fuel – which is a source of increased greenhouse gas emissions. So we understand instinctively if it were added to current economic activity, a plan for ecological investment, even publicly funded and not for profit, would be incompatible with the need to reduce emissions at a global level by 2015 at the latest, and to reduce them by at least 95% by 2050 in developed countries. Furthermore, the countries of the Global South are expected at the same time to equip themselves on a large scale with clean technologies, and these will also need energy input. The conclusion is inescapable. The constraints cannot be respected unless the investments necessary for a new energy system go hand in hand with a radical reduction of energy consumption in developed countries.

What level of reduction? In a study produced at the request of Greenpeace, experts on thermodynamics at the University of Stuttgart estimated that for the EU to make the transition to the use of renewables, if it is done in parallel with the abandonment of nuclear power, it would be necessary to reduce the consumption of primary energy by 37%, to reduce the demand for heat by 50% (by insulating buildings) and to reduce the demand in the transport sector by 40%. According to this report, a reduction of primary consumption in particular is indispensable in order to avoid having recourse to nuclear power.[138] These figures are based on the hypothesis of a 60% reduction in emissions – probably insufficient with regard to the physical constraints of climate stabilisation. It is therefore no exaggeration to emphasise the idea that, in the coming 40 years, a 50% reduction in energy consumption is the condition to be fulfilled for renewables to take over from fossil fuels and nuclear power in Europe. In the USA, the reduction must be even more draconian. This is not impossible contrary to what may be believed. The fact that the average American consumes twice as much as the average European – with a GDP per individual not significantly larger – indicates the possibility of very substantial reductions.

Nevertheless, it is clear that reducing energy usage by 50% - 75% is not possible merely by concentrating on unnecessary usage (excessive lighting or heating, for example) or immediate increases in energy efficiency – the time limit is too short and the effort would be too great. In order for it to work properly, it is imperative to move to the next stage via a planned reduction in the processing of materials – producing less and transporting less. It is beyond the scope of this volume to quantify this reduction by sector, this would need the input of a multi-disciplinary team. We shall confine ourselves here to listing a series of activities which are useless (advertising), harmful (arms manufacture), or unsustainable (production of millions of vehicles, relocation of food production under the auspices of agri-business) – without taking into account the growing mass of gadgets which travel thousands of kilometres before ending up in supermarkets. Other reductions could be rapidly achieved by imposing norms of product durability, forbidding road transport beyond a certain distance and stimulating collective use of facilities at the local level.

The Left is ill at ease with all this. At worst it ignores the problem. At best, it is on the defensive; 'Yes, but we can reduce material production without threatening the way of life of the majority'. This argument, which suggests that only 'the rich' would need to change their way of life and their way of consumption, does not hold water. It is a final example of the old idea that, with regard to the environment and a certain number of other questions, 'We'll see after the Revolution'. That idea is obsolete. According to the campaign 'Don't eat the world',[139] 44% - 57% of greenhouse gas emissions are caused by the current mode of production, distribution and consumption of agricultural and forestry products. This figure is obtained by adding strictly agricultural emissions (11% - 15%), emissions caused by deforestation (15% - 18%), handling, transport and storage of foodstuffs (15% - 20%) and organic residues. These figures are sufficient to indicate that the struggle to stabilise the climate at the best possible level cannot be limited to expropriating the expropriators and polluters. The change in property relations is only the necessary – but insufficient – condition for a very profound social change, involving substantial modifications in society's modes of consumption and mobility. These modifications – travelling differently, eating less meat and more seasonal vegetables, for instance – should be undertaken immediately, because time is short and there are immediate implications. This can be done, as the modifications make use of cultural and ideological mechanisms which enjoy a certain autonomy in relation to the productive base of society. The ideology of the dominant class is the dominant ideology, not the only possible ideology. This is why, in my view, a response that takes the offensive in regard to the question of quality and standard of living is more appropriate than the defensive response common on the Left. It is a matter of taking the bull by the horns, to dare to say that, generally speaking, producing, transporting and consuming less in developed countries has become a necessary condition for a better life.

It goes without saying that this necessary condition will be far from sufficient if it does not also take into account the fight against social inequality. It must therefore be accompanied by a reduction in the length of the working week without pay cuts and with a reduction in work intensity, and the redistribution of wealth through the taxation, the cancelling of illegitimate public debts, the expansion of the public sector and by making basic services available free of charge. Without all this, millions of people will remain unemployed, millions of others will lose their jobs and a whole section of society will continue to be deprived of basic goods and services. But the Left has some answers to these questions. Marx said; 'In the final analysis, all economics comes down to an economics of time'. To assert the necessity of producing and consuming less is to reclaim the time to live and to live better. It is to open a fundamental debate in society about social time management, about who needs what, why and in what quantities. It is to awaken the collective desire for a world without war, where we work less and in a different way, where there is less pollution, where we develop social relations, where there are substantial improvements in well-being, in public health, education and participation in the democratic process. This would be a world in which the associated producers would learn again to rationally regulate their interchange with Nature. This world would not be less rich than today's world, as the Right claims, nor 'just rich enough for the majority of the population', as some on the Left claim, It would be infinitely more meaningful, less stressed, less hurried – in a word, richer.

This anti-productivist concept is decisive as a basis for the Left's response to the climate challenge. We will see in due course that it differs from the policy of Zero Growth in that it puts the emphasis on changes in the sphere of production, in other words on the collective and structural solutions which alone would permit humanity to regain control of its existence. For now, let us concentrate on this conclusion – a drastic reduction of energy consumption in developed countries is the *sine qua non* to achieve what is necessary, and this reduction implies in turn some reduction of production, as well as in transport of materials. Now, this is completely incompatible with the laws of capitalism. In a certain sense, it could be argued that the problem of accumulation is even greater than that of the profit motive. Capitalism can if necessary adapt to a plan (it can do so in times of war).[140] It can tolerate governments increasing taxes on company profits for a limited period in order to prevent social unrest (as Roosevelt did with the New Deal in the 1930s). But it cannot function without growth.

The economist Schumpeter said, 'A stationary capitalism is a contradiction in terms'. The reason is simple and re-unites the concepts of accumulation and profit which, for convenience, we have analysed separately. Competition encourages every owner of capital to replace workers with more productive machines, to turn an average profit into a large profit. This race for higher profits via technology inevitably implies greater and greater quantities of goods thrust into circulation in search of consumers who have the means and the desire to buy them. Certainly the intensive use of energy and materials has diminished (production becomes more and more immaterial), but this reduction is more than offset by the increase in the volume of production.[141] In his analysis of the specific case of the motor car, Matthew Patterson concludes euphemistically that attempts to produce green cars are 'highly problematic and probably impossible'.[142] This is obvious common sense, but common sense sometimes disappears in certain scientific studies. For instance, researchers at the renowned German Aerospace Centre (DLR) have proposed a projection of electricity needs for 2050 based on the hypothesis of a linear relation between the growth of gross national product (GNP) per individual and the rise in energy efficiency. Now, this can obviously not be infinite, so we would end up with the absurd conclusion that raw materials can be processed without energy.[143]

The system is based on accumulation, and can only reduce its material production by periodic crises of over-production. These do slightly reduce the pressure on the environment, but they operate blindly, causing poverty, increased inequality and waste of resources. Recent history furnishes a striking example; according to the International Energy Agency, the 2009 recession resulted in a 3% reduction in global emissions. At what cost? Let us take the example of Spain, it is crystal clear. CO_2 emissions in the first six months of the year were reduced by 16.9% in comparison with the corresponding period in 2008, but the number of unemployed increased by 50%, and a figure of 17% or even greater was forecast for 2010 by some institutions. This is no cause for rejoicing, especially since the respite for the planet will only be temporary; once capitalism regains its cost-effectiveness, it will continue its headlong rush.

We must therefore not be misled by the progress of renewables and green products in general. A capitalist response to climate change inevitably takes the form of numerous capitalist competitors driving accumulation, which is shown in growing needs for energy. Thus the IEA invariably counts on a doubling of energy needs by 2030. Indeed, all its scenarios are based on this dogma. In this context, renewables, which make a profit (with or without a public subsidy), start by being used alongside fossil fuels, instead of replacing them. In the field of consumption, economists often speak of the rebound effect – because low-energy bulbs use less electricity than incandescent bulbs, more are installed. Now, the fundamental origin of this phenomenon can be traced to level of production. This is shown for example by the Desertec project, which made headline news.

A grandiose project costing 400 billion euros, Desertec aims to concentrate solar radiation from the Sahara in order to produce within the next 20 years up to 15% of the EU's electricity needs. Continuous electrical current is to be produced via cables. In itself this project is far from being absurd, but, within the productivist framework, it is part of a headlong rush, which does not lead to any structural solution. Within this framework, in fact, the supply of electricity will create demand, based on the assumption that the number of equipment being sold will continue to increase. Because of this, the gains in efficiency are more than offset by the increase in production and the energy efficiency of products will increase in general by 1.5% - 2% per annum, creating a larger profit for the electricity companies. If Desertec ever becomes operational, it will be able to cover a substantial part of this increased supply, but it will not radically shrink the use of fossil fuels.

The fact is that the logic of capitalism is chiefly responsible for the climate tipping-point which evidently has major implications for the 'Third World'. In fact, the model of development which subordinates the economies of the South to the imperatives of accumulation, within the framework of globalisation of production and trade, is completely incompatible with the necessary reduction of emissions from 15% - 30% by 2020 (2050 for Africa) discussed in the previous chapter. This objective can only be achieved by means of endogenous development, responsive to the needs of the majority of the population – linked, therefore, to agrarian reform in favour of peasant agriculture and to a restructuring of production in favour of the local market. That is to say that supporting the right to human development and stopping climate change means taking measures against the local dominant classes, who use the pretext of the right to development to block any restriction on the use of fossil fuels, to plunder natural resources, take over the forests and export agricultural and industrial products at low prices to the markets of the developed world.

At this point the realisation of energy potential comes up against the laws of profit and accumulation, so that it is tempting to unhesitatingly pronounce a final verdict; stabilisation of the climate at the least dangerous level possible represents the squaring of the circle for capitalism. But let us not be too hasty. History encourages us to be prudent. The system is flexible and this has more than once enabled it to thwart the predictions of its adversaries in order to extricate itself from dead-end situations, even it means postponing future problems. At the time of writing, the ruling class claims to be aware of the danger. To consolidate our analysis and to define more clearly what awaits us, we must undertake a concrete examination of the climate policies of different governments.

Chapter Seven
KYOTO – A HAPHAZARD POLICY

In 2007, the IPCC and Al Gore receive the Nobel Peace Prize, while George Bush's position is defeated at the Bali climate summit and Australia does an about-face by ratifying the Kyoto protocol. In 2008, the G8 declares that it is in favour of a 50% reduction in global emissions by 2050 while the EU adopts an 'energy-climate package'. In 2009, we see a new G8 resolution this time in favour of an 80% reduction in developed countries, and Obama promises in his election campaign to reduce US emissions by 80% between now and 2050. Are these clear signs that the developed world is prepared to subscribe to a world-wide effort to avoid an irreversible catastrophe?

The wind seems to have changed. Most governments and heads of state declare that they are fully aware of the gravity of the situation. The financial press castigates those who hesitate and exhorts them to fall in line. 'Business lobby demands emissions goals' was a headline in the Financial Times during the Bali conference[144]. But there is many a slip between cup and lip.

It is not possible to understand climate politics without returning to the starting point, the Kyoto Protocol. This document, adopted in 1997 under the aegis of the United Nations, exhorts industrialised countries to reduce their emissions by 5.2% between 2008 and 2012, in relation to 1990.[145] In fact, due to the withdrawal of the US, only a third of this target will be realised.[146] What is more, although these targets are inadequate, attempts to meet them are further weakened by the fact that the reduction of emissions due to reduced energy wastage or transition to renewables are put on the same level as increases in carbon absorption resulting from forestry planting.

The reduction of emissions is structural while the increase in absorption is necessarily limited to the longevity of the trees. Finally, thanks to neo-liberal globalisation, emissions from air and maritime transport (2% of the global total, rising rapidly) are not taken into account. In short, as they say, 'Kyoto is peanuts'.

Nevertheless, these 'peanuts' have been far from useless to the polluters. The Protocol has effectively served as the testing ground for three 'mechanisms of flexibility': the Clean Development Mechanism (CDM), the Joint Implementation Mechanism (JIM)[147] and the EU Emissions Trading System (EU ETS). Officially, they aim to facilitate the achievement of the targets. In fact they are more a way of evading them and turning them into sources of profit.

The exchange of carbon emissions allowances enables businesses that meet or exceed their reduction targets to sell their right to emit a corresponding amount of tonnes of carbon. The Clean Development Mechanism offers developed countries the chance to replace part of their target by the purchase of 'emission credits' – a variety of entitlements generated by investments allowing the reduction of emissions in the countries of the Global South, according to the projections. The Joint Implementation Mechanism is a variant of the Clean Development Mechanism in the former Warsaw Pact countries which are considered to be 'in transition'. A clear understanding of these mechanisms and the way they operate is fundamental for taking the measure of the grandiose declarations evoking reductions of 50% or more by 2050.

The three mechanisms imply the creation of a carbon market which would allow them to inter-connect and trade carbon quotas,[148] is the keystone here. In practice countries subject to a requirement to reduce emissions draw up a list of industries which emit a lot of CO_2 such as thermal power stations, cement works, steel works, glass works, brick works, oil refineries and paper mills.

At the outset, each business receives a certain number of units of CO_2, or emission rights (one right = one tonne). This figure is negotiated with government. Once validated by the public authorities it constitutes the limit of authorised emissions (a quota). Then the businesses inform the government annually of the amount of CO_2 emitted and have this figure verified by an independent auditor. For every tonne emitted the business must register a unit of emission and if the limit is exceeded there is a penalty.[149] To avoid the penalty businesses exceeding their quota may buy the quotas offered for sale by those who have not exceeded the limit.

Currently, the only realisation of this plan of action is the EU Emissions Trading System (ETS), which encompasses 11,500 units of production[150] and covers two periods: 2005 – 2007 and 2008 – 2012. From the outset, the mechanism was weighted in favour of businesses. During the first period, in fact, emission rights were distributed free.[151] Also, too many rights were allocated at the start so the basis of calculations for subsequent reductions was distorted.

The Commission would have us believe that the difference between the quotas distributed and the actual emissions proves the environmental efficiency of the system, but it is well known that governments have been remarkably lax in the distribution of rights, in order not to damage the competitiveness of 'their' businesses. This has led to four consequences:

1) The price of a tonne of CO_2 fell drastically at the beginning of 2005, from 30 to 10 euros a tonne;
2) Owners of businesses preferred to buy emission rights rather than investing in clean technologies;
3) Businesses which needed them bought rights cheaply;
4) Those with rights to sell made a lucrative trade, since emission rights had been distributed for free.

A few examples may serve as an illustration. In 2005, the European steel industry pocketed more that 480 million euros of exceptional profit (1% of the turnover of the cast steel industry) by selling its surplus tonnes of CO_2. This is far from being an isolated case and even oil companies have made the most of this golden opportunity via rights allocated to refineries.[152] Electricity companies too, because the market has been liberalised and they have a 'captive audience', have been able to reflect the market price of carbon quotas in the bills to customers even though their quotas were distributed free of charge! On the other hand, smaller organisations such as universities and hospitals, who had received too small a quota, were obliged to purchase them.[153]

In Germany, the official organ of the fight against cartels accused the RWE electricity company of manipulating the market. The company had pocketed an excess profit of 1.8 billion euros. RWE's argument in defence of this was that the value of the assets should be reflected in the price level[154] and that 'this is the only way climate politics can make progress via energy saving mechanisms and investments in the most efficient sites of production'.[155] It is the same story in the UK where electricity companies have made an extra profit of £800 million. According to the investment bank UBS, the first phase of ETS 'has probably contributed to a rise in electricity prices from 10 to 20 euros per MW/h, with a significant redistribution of wealth away from consumers towards the producers shared out among the electricity companies'.[157]

Contrary to what is claimed by RWE, these excess profits have not been invested in 'more efficient production sites'. RWE itself acknowledges that it is constructing the biggest lignite-based power station in the world.[158] As for the steel sector, it is only contributing 45 million euros a year (less than

0.5% of its turnover) to the ULCOS research programme in 'low carbon' technologies.[159]

The conclusion, obviously, is that the policy of trade in rights was supposed to facilitate the fight against climate change but has, in fact, reinforced the sectors which have the largest emissions of greenhouse gases and this holds back the fight against climate change by delaying as much as possible the abandonment of fossil fuels. The two other mechanisms of flexibility exacerbate the situation. The EU has decided that, during the second phase of ETS, the trade of quotas should be linked to the Clean Development Mechanism (CDM) and the Joint Implementation Mechanism (JIM). In other words, apart from exceptions, a carbon credit generated by 'clean' investment in the Third World or Eastern Europe[160] is the equivalent of one ETS right to emission and is negotiable on the European emission rights market.

To see the effects of this link we will concentrate on the CDM, which is much more important than the JIM. Its aim, theoretically, is not to undermine incentives to reduce carbon emissions at the heart of the EU. It has no effect in practice, since the volumes of emission authorised are so large. While annual emissions from Member States were required to be reduced by about 130 million tonnes in the course of the second phase of ETS (2008 – 2012), 280 million tonnes of carbon in the form of credits have been authorised to enter the EU every year.[161] In the worst case, if it were not for the administrative complications of the system, businesses could divert the whole of their efforts towards the countries of the Global South![162]

The inter-connection between the mechanisms offers enormous opportunities to multi-national corporations. A study carried out for the European Federation of Trade Unions[163] correctly observes that, because of the mechanisms of flexibility, CO_2 is no longer a waste product but a by-product, and its commercial potential co-determines the industrial strategy of businesses. Because of this, the multinationals can alternate their main production sites and CO_2-producing sites in order to maximise their profits according to the relative prices of carbon and other products. A corner of this veil was lifted when Martin Pecina, director of the anti-trust organisation UOHS in the Czech Republic, accused the largest steel manufacturer in the world, Mittal Steel, of reducing local steel production to benefit its factories in Kazakhstan (which does not subscribe to the ETS), in order to be able to sell its Czech quotas in Western Europe.[164]

Kyoto stipulates that credits should be generated from investments that would not have normally been made. This is known as the 'principle of additionality' in the CDM. In practice, it is virtually ignored. In its factory at Tubarao, Brazil, ArcelorMittal made an investment in order to produce electricity by burning gases in a blast furnace. This commonplace investment would probably have been approved at some point, as it would have reduced energy costs. Nevertheless the proposal, accepted by the executive office of the CDM, will provide the multinational firm 430,000 tonnes worth of tradable credits.[165] In another region of Brazil, burning charcoal instead of coke will generate millions of tonnes of coke between 2008 and 2015.[166]

To the extent to which a 'clean' investment would have been made in any case, the credits it generates are almost free, just like the rights distributed during the first phase of the ETS.[167] The trade of rights is therefore a very profitable business. If the rights do not cover the cost of emissions from subsidiaries in the EU, investments in these subsidiaries where the technology is more advanced which would therefore be more costly than in countries of the Global South can be avoided. The rights can be sold on the European carbon market. As ETS quotas are more expensive than credits, a significant surplus can be gained.

According to an analyst from Fortis Bank, the difference in cost was 4% in 2007, so that the opportunity for excess profit was evaluated globally at a billion dollars per annum.[168] Rights and credits can be accumulated for sale until the price is right so that the carbon market becomes a new speculative market.

As its name indicates, the CDM is supposed at the very least to contribute to the transfer of clean technologies needed by the Global South. This is far from the reality however. In 2008, African countries only received 27 of the 1,150 CDM projects existing in 49 countries.[169] More than 50% of projects are located in China. The logic of this is that the primary aim of the CDM, in reality, is not to reduce emissions. It is there on the one hand to produce maximum credits at minimum cost in order to maximise profits, and on the other hand to reduce the cost of transition. China is ideal from this point of view. Its industry is highly developed but at the same time has very out of date equipment and is a major emitter of CO_2, so it can be modernised at low cost.

If the Chinese stock of electrical power stations were as efficient as that of Japan, it would consume 21% less fuel, which would mean a vast reservoir of 'clean' investments, and therefore CDM credits. It is a similar tale in the steel industry. In 2004, China produced 273 million tonnes of steel. If this production had been achieved by emitting 1.4 tonnes of CO_2 per tonne of steel, as in the EU, Chinese emissions would have been reduced by 546Mt per tonne, or a twentieth of the global emission total.[170]

What do the investors do? They calculate the share which can be cancelled for less than 10 dollars per tonne and rub their hands. So as to be sure not to miss a trick, Mittal decided to finance a plan by the UNDP[171] consisting of an investment of 1.7 million dollars to create 'technical centres for the CDM'. The aim of this operation was to attract the projects in no less than twelve provinces,[172] a modest investment when one thinks of the huge excess profits derived from the sale of credits. True, these investments in the Chinese electrical and steel industries effectively allow a reduction in emissions even though they are inspired by the profit motive, but other cases are more debatable. For instance, the exploitation of coal bed methane qualifies as a CDM project. Beijing has significant reserves of coal bed methane and 15 projects were launched in 2007, in collaboration with foreign firms such as Chevron.[173]

The breakdown of projects by type of technology holds as many surprises as does their geographical location. In 2005, 64% of CDM credits sold on the market derived from the destruction of the gas HFC-23.[174] This gas with the outlandish name is the waste product of a refrigerant with an irradiative power 11,700 times greater than that of CO_2. Eliminating this gas qualifies as a CDM project with the destruction of one tonne (it costs one euro per tonne) generating 11,700 credits whose sale price is about 11 euros. Consequently Asia has experienced a boom in the manufacture of refrigerants. The output of credits for destruction of the waste products has become more profitable than the sale of the product!

In view of the scandal, it was decided that factories built after 2000 could no longer profit from the goose that lays the golden egg – but it is still laying! A Swiss NGO submitted a request for a review that the CDM seems in no hurry to respond to.[175] In any case the capitalist market offers a wide variety of similar opportunities and the world is full of shrewd operators ready to exploit them.[176]

Where does the climate fit in all this? Proponents of the Mechanisms of Flexibility argue that since CO_2 travels rapidly round the planet all reductions of emissions, wherever they occur, contribute to the objectives. This is true, but with two caveats. Firstly, this does not justify the fact that the EU has declared that a CDM credit and an ETS quota are equal. In the case of ETS, a tonne of carbon which has really been emitted has ceased to exist, so that an emission right becomes available. In the case of credits, on the other hand, a tonne of carbon which may be emitted in the future is meant to be prevented by a clean investment. It is not the same thing. Who can guarantee, for instance, that the scenario of reference is correct? Secondly, the HFC-23 affair demonstrates that a large proportion of credits does not guarantee any structural effort to save the climate.

What proportion are we talking about? A fifth, according to The Guardian a few years ago;[177] about 60%, according to a more recent estimate by two researchers at Stanford University. They targeted in particular the new Chinese electrical installations – wind-turbines, hydraulic or natural gas power stations – which all claim recognition within the framework of the CDM. According to the regulations currently in force, such projects can effectively obtain credits, as a proportion of the reduction of emissions in relation to waste products from coal-fired power stations. Project by project, 'additionality' seems to be respected. The researchers estimate, however, that, on a global scale, these installations would have been built anyway because China has enormous electricity needs and enough coal to meet the demand.[178]

To complete the overview of current climate policies, we will briefly discuss the application of norms, penalties and incentives in favour of green technologies in sectors not covered by ETS: construction, transport, agriculture and forestry. To analyse the entire raft of measures would stray too far from our topic, but there is one revealing example, the neo-liberal policy of allowances/bonuses for photovoltaic panels.

Following the German example, one of the many successive governments of Belgium has encouraged individuals to install photovoltaic panels by offering them benefits. On offer is an investment bonus of 20%, with a ceiling of 3,500 euros; a tax reduction of 40%, with a ceiling of 3,400 euros (with the payment spread over two years, this means a double profit) and 'Green Certificates' guaranteed for 15 years at a minimum of 65 euros.[179] For an installation generating 2,550 KWh of electricity a year – the consumption of a household[180] – the investment is around 17,500 euros, including VAT. The fortunate owners will receive the maximum bonus (3,500 euros), gain a double profit from the tax reduction, sell electricity for about 430 euros per annum and gain 17 Green Certificates a year, all of which will net them between 1,105 and 1,564 euros. The investment will be paid off within four years.

For well-off property owners, the game is worth it because after those four years the sale of electricity and certificates will continue to bring in 1,500 euros per annum for a further 11 years. Furthermore, the value of the property will increase, especially if the project of grading buildings according to their ecological impact comes into effect. The cost – bonuses, tax reductions and certificates – is met entirely from public funds. Electricity suppliers, who are under a legal obligation to buy certificates, pass the cost on to the consumers, so that those who have to pay through the nose are tenants and owners of smaller properties who pay more for their electricity.[181]

And what environmental impact does all this have? This question can be answered by comparing the social cost per tonne of CO_2 emissions with the cost of preventing emissions through publicly funded investments to insulate a gable end, thermal solar panels and photovoltaic panels. The most efficient method is insulation of the gable end. This saves 85 tonnes of CO_2 in 40 years at a cost of 131 euros per tonne whereas thermal and/or photovoltaic installations only save 7.8 and 9.8 tonnes respectively in 20 years at a cost of 768 and 856 euros per tonne respectively. The cost of public subsidies for each MWh saved would be 376 euros for the photovoltaic, 175 euros for thermal solar panels and just 6.55 euros for insulating the gable end. Clearly, the system of bonuses encourages less efficient solutions.[182]

In varying degrees, this haphazard policy is followed by all governments who seem to have suddenly forgotten that cost-effectiveness is the major criterion of their climate policies.

But the contradiction is more apparent than real. The policy's real aim is not to combat global warming as efficiently as possible but to promote the development of eco-industry, to offer a market to small and medium-sized businesses and to fill the order books of green manufacturers (who adapt the prices of their solar panels according to the country and according to the bonuses). Meanwhile, governments get an 'eco-image' and distribute gifts to well-off taxpayers and voters. The same criticism applies in other fields, such as incentives to buy hybrid cars.

Whether at the general level of carbon markets or at the national level of incentives to clean technologies, the result is the same. The policies followed until now within the framework of the Kyoto Protocol combine a partial rationality in the service of profit and global irrationality, so that their environmental inefficiency remains. At the same time they reinforce social inequalities, not only between North and South but also within the societies of the North and those of the South. It is in the light of this that the next chapter will examine new developments in climate politics.

Chapter Eight
'FEET GLUED TO THE ACCELERATOR'

Faced with the scientific consensus and with obvious evidence of global warming, governments are trying to give the impression that they are implementing a more ambitious and long-term climate strategy than Kyoto. In this chapter, we shall first analyse the climate policy of the EU, then that of the USA.

At the beginning of 2008, the European Commission proposed an 'energy-climate package' to the European Parliament and the member states. It was adopted at the end of the year, subject to a series of modifications. Its aims are a 20% reduction in emissions by 2020 (30% in the case of a satisfactory international agreement), a 20% rise in energy efficiency and a target of 20% renewable energy – of which 10% is to be biofuels in the transport sector. The EU therefore boasts that it is showing the way to a post-Kyoto world. But in fact the package is a load of hot air. Five observations will suffice to expose it.

Firstly, the package does not measure up to the conclusions to be drawn from the IPCC reports. As we have seen, according to the IPCC, developed countries ought to reduce their emissions by between 25% - 40% by 2020, in order not to go too far past the limit of 2°C rise in temperature. In the name of the precautionary principle, given the uncertainty of 'non-linear phenomena', this 40% should be considered a minimum. The EU is very much below this target. Furthermore, the 'package' is not even in line with the EU's own objective of a rise in temperature of below 2°C, adopted in 1996. Apparently the left hand of a Eurocrat doesn't know what the right hand is doing.

Secondly, the original 'package' planned to auction rights instead of distributing them for free. Yet many member states and industrial sectors insisted on demanding that 'businesses subject to international competition' should continue to receive their rights for free, in order to prevent 'carbon leakage', in other words the relocation of businesses which emit large amounts of carbon.[183] According to Karsten Neuhoff, economist and senior research associate at Cambridge University, UK, the amount of EU GNP attributable to intensive carbon activities is of the order of 1%.[184] There was therefore no real cause for alarm, but the industry bosses succeeded in their demands and the relevant sectors will receive up to 100% of their quotas for free. Only a fifth of the quotas for industry will be auctioned in 2013.

A word about electricity suppliers who are a special case. There is no need to raise the spectre of relocation or outsourcing (it is impossible for the electricity sold in Europe to be produced in China). The rights will be auctioned in 2013. But companies such as E.ON, RWE and Suez have no need to worry because there is nothing to stop them passing on the market price of their rights to the consumer. The result will probably be a rise in tariffs of 10% - 15% by 2020[185] and that is without taking into account other factors in the rise of electricity prices. Furthermore, electricity suppliers in the former Warsaw Pact countries, which make massive use of coal-fired power stations, are benefitting from exceptions. In 2013 they will only have to pay for 30% of their quotas – this will rise to 100% in 2020.

Thirdly, new gases and new economic sectors are being added to the EU Emissions Trading System (ETS) which will also cover CO_2 emissions from the petro-chemical industry, from the production of ammonia and aluminium, as well as various emissions of nitrous oxide or perfluorocarbon. The leaders of these sectors have not complained.[186] Why? Because they hope to benefit from an over-allocation of rights, like their colleagues in other sectors and line their pockets while making fine speeches about the planet. 'A low carbon economy could constitute a great opportunity if the transition is well-managed,' said Alain Perroy, head of the European Federation of Chemical Industries (CEFIC) as he greeted the climate decisions of the Council of Europe.[187]

Fourthly, all industrial sectors, whether old or new, included in the ETS (jointly responsible for about 40% of EU emissions) will see their allocated quota of rights reduced annually by 1.74%, which will mean a cumulative reduction of 21% by 2020, in comparison with 2005. This principle of a linear reduction is positive, but the rate of 1.74% does not indicate a superhuman effort when compared to the spontaneous fall in energy intensity. In the US, which does not have a reputation for abstemiousness in this field, the reduction of energy consumption in specific technological fields, for example, was 1.9% per annum between 1980 and 1995.[188]

Fifthly, for the first time, the 'energy-climate package' includes a reduction target of 10% between 2012 and 2020 in transport, construction and agriculture – sectors not covered by the ETS. These sectors are responsible for 60% of EU emissions and the potential for energy economy is very significant. But there is no question of Brussels drastically cutting back on HGVs, or taking on agribusiness or taking a public initiative to insulate all homes. This is why the 'package' has fixed such a high target in the field of biofuels – a target which implies massive imports from the Global South. This is also why it has given the green light to the purchase of pollution rights from the CDM. In this sector, within the period, up to 70% of emission reductions would be replaced by imported credits!

This question of the purchase of credits is decisive. In effect, the more the ruling class is convinced of the necessity of acting against the climate tipping-point, the more it tends to transform obligations to make real reductions in the North into projections of reductions in the South, affecting to ignore the fact that many of these reductions will not occur.

The Stern report proposed to suppress completely all hindrances to the Clean Development Mechanism (CDM) so as to get a 40-fold increase in volume and to reduce the price of credits.[189] The report argued in particular for credits to be generated not only by planting trees but also by protecting existing forests. The Bali climate conference followed its example, opening the door to the UN-REDD programme, subsequently transformed into the REDD+ programme.[190] Some NGOs were delighted at what they saw as measures to the preserve natural resources.

Of course the tropical rainforest must be saved, and this includes the tropical rainforest that global warming is changing from a carbon sink into a carbon source.[191] But it must be saved for its own sake and for that of its inhabitants, not so that big business can obtain cheap credits which will allow it to continue destroying health, the climate and the environment. The key point is that a credit deriving from the non-exploitation of an existing forest would cost less than five dollars which is why certain industrialists have suddenly changed into defenders of the green lungs of the planet.

'But you are criticising everything! If businesses are defending the tropical rainforest, so much the better!' This is an objection that will be raised in certain quarters. In the logic of capitalism, however, this 'defence' consists of appropriating the resources of the forest at the expense of indigenous communities who are accused of destroying the ecosystem that they created.

There are numerous examples. The case of Rio Bravo Conservation and Management Area (RCB MAS), demonstrates not only the logic of capitalism, but also the direction in which certain NGOs are heading. This RBCMA is a vast project of carbon capture, protecting a zone of 53,000 hectares in Belize. Programme for Belize, the initiator of the project and owner of the land, is a large American environmental NGO which was given thousands of hectares by the American multinational Coca-Cola.

With the financial support of a consortium of US energy businesses, the RBCMA project hopes to capture ten million tonnes of CO_2 within 40 years and sell the corresponding credits at 2.2 dollars a tonne. Since the Ichaiche Maya indigenous people balk at abandoning their traditional mode of production based on gathering and nomadic agriculture, the NGO has the area patrolled by armed vigilantes to keep them off the land. Confrontations are frequent. One of the coordinators of the project has stated: 'In our capacity as private owners of the land, we are obliged to protect natural resources – we have a mission to accomplish'. It seems the road to hell is paved with good – green – intentions![192]

Although it has not (yet) opened the door wide to 'forestry' credits, the EU is relying more and more on the CDM – this 'trade of indulgences', as Italian environmentalist Professor Giorgio Nebbia has described it.[193] In the absence of an international agreement for 2012-2020 (with the option of a reduction of 20%), businesses included in the ETS could use the balance of their credits for the period 2008-2012. As we have seen, the import ceiling for this phase is very high. So much so that, as the Commission itself acknowledges that the credits for 2008-2012 could cover more than a third of the reductions called for between 2012 and 2020.[194] In the case of an international agreement, up to 50% of the reduction in emissions corresponding to the new target of 30% could be covered by credits.

Let us recap. The EU is committed to a 20% (or 30%) reduction in emissions, while 40% is needed. For big business, which is responsible for 40% of the emissions, the annual rate of reduction is less than the annual rate of improvement in energy efficiency and a third of the reduction could be replaced by purchase of credits. In the construction, agriculture and transport sectors accounting for 60% of total emissions, the purchase of these credits could replace up to 70% of reductions. In total, therefore, more than half the effort of reduction could be achieved outside the EU. Now, more that 60% of these credits do not correspond to any real reductions, and some of them (forestry credits) do not correspond to structural reductions. Take a paper and pencil and do the maths: if the potential of credits were fully utilised, the EU would only reduce its emissions by 14%, instead of 20%, in eight years. The whole thing is a hoax.

This is being done in full knowledge of the facts. In a report for the environmental department of the European Parliament, the consultancy Ecofys had warned – 'In order to reach the target of 2°C the EU must adopt a reduction target of at least 30% by 2020 (in comparison with 1990) and take additional action to reduce emissions in developing countries'. Very importantly, the report's authors placed particular emphasis on the fact that

CDM credits cannot replace domestic actions.[195]

The IPCC states that between now and 2050, countries in the North must reduce their emissions by 80%-95%. It adds that those countries of the Global South, according to projections, should divert theirs by 15%-30% thanks to clean investments. It goes without saying that, if the reductions corresponding to these investments are added to the credit of developing countries, either the countries of the Global South will be cheated, or the final account will not tally, as some reductions will have been counted twice. The Council of Europe and the Members of the European Parliament paid no attention to this warning and former French president Nicolas Sarkozy, in his capacity as EU president, actually bragged to the media; 'This is an historic moment, there is no other continent on earth which has such strict regulations and frankly it was much easier to achieve than we had thought'.[196] For good reason!

The US is going in a similar direction. This was already beginning to emerge in early 2007[197] but it became obvious after Barack Obama became US president. The Waxman-Markey Bill on Climate Law, adopted by Congress in June 2009, recommended a reduction of emissions by 80% between then and 2050. The presidential spin-doctors did their best to make this figure look impressive but it was a smokescreen.

Firstly, since the US is the greatest polluter on the planet, it should be the first to aim for a reduction of at least 95%. Secondly, it should be noted that the year it refers back to is 2005, whereas the IPCC's recommendation of 80%-95% uses 1990 as a point of reference. In fact, between these two dates, CO_2 emissions from fossil fuel in the US have risen from 5.8 billion tonnes to 7 billion tonnes. The Waxman-Markey Bill proposes a reduction of 17% from today's levels. Not only is this target very much lower than that of the 25% - 40% recommended by the IPCC, it is also below the target which the US should have reached in 2012 if it had ratified the Kyoto Protocol.

Just as happened with the original version of the EU 'package', the electoral promises of Obama have been subjected to intense pressure from industrial lobbies which deemed them not liberal enough. As in the EU, the lobbies concentrated on two points: the auctioning of rights and emission credits. During his first presidential election campaign, Obama promised that all rights would be sold at auction. The resulting revenue, he pledged, would be used to fund a vast programme of research and development into renewables and also to alleviate the cost of energy transition for the disadvantaged.

Instead, the draft adopted by Congress allowed for free distribution of 85% of rights. As in the EU, rather than the polluters being penalised, they were left free to do business and gain advantages at the expense of the community. Emission credits could be derived not only from clean investments in the Global South but from the creation of 'carbon sinks' in the US by planting trees and various agricultural practices (whose long-term effect is uncertain) designed to increase the storage of organic carbon in the soil.[198]

On a global scale, American businesses could use up to 2 billion dollars credits deriving from these offset mechanisms. The handout is so generous that, if full use were made of it, industry could avoid reducing its own emissions until 2026. British journalist and environmental campaigner George Monbiot dryly noted that this Bill 'is riddled with so many loopholes and concessions that the Bill's measures might not offset the emissions from the paper it's printed on'.[199]

The obvious similarities between US and EU policies[200] do not result from a recognition of a shared responsibility on the part of the powerful in the face of the challenge, but from the fact that the ruling classes all over the world are obliged to admit the necessity of a voluntaristic public policy and more or less recognise the European 'model' as the path to follow in the neo-liberal context. As a senior executive of the multinational company DuPont put it several years ago: 'Economies will have to adapt. The US would make a mistake if it isolated itself from these pressures. When reality catches up with us, we would be behind schedule and our competitors would be ahead of us in the development and use of soft technologies'.[201] So it is not cooperation that is the order of the day, but unrestrained competition between groups, between sectors and between countries because capitalists worldwide demand that their state defends their interests.

In this context, the position taken by the US is revealing. Barack Obama's *Plan to Make America a Global Energy Leader* is the title of the energy-climate section of Barack Obama's first presidential campaign.[202] Its guiding principle is not to avoid catastrophe but to safeguard America's leading position in world affairs, especially in the field of energy. In this document, Bush was blamed for having increased oil dependence on producing countries with hostile regimes and for having led the US into an impasse in which it had not only lost complete control of Latin America but was also weaker in relation to the EU and China.

The climate policy of Obama fits into this framework. In effect, it constitutes the start of a considerable change of geo-strategic direction, aimed at re-establishing the hegemony of the US empire in a context of increased competition between imperialist powers and new, rising capitalist powers.

This geo-strategic approach is especially obvious in Obama's stance with regard to large 'emergent' nations. It should be understood that the refusal to accept a compulsory emissions quota was not the only reason for Bush's opposition to Kyoto. Another reason was that the Protocol imposed no similar conditions on the 'Famous Five' – China, India, Brazil, Mexico and South Africa. On this point, the present incumbent of the White House is in agreement with the previous one, but does not share his tactics. In Obama's view, it was the US refusal of any domestic quotas which has played into the hands of India and China, while the EU has profited from the US refusal to set itself up as the leader in the climate field and to take the lead in the renewables market.

Obama wants to dislodge the EU from this position. To achieve this he has to take the reins of post-Kyoto negotiation, for the new agreement to correspond with the interests of the US. Since the previous US Administration was discredited on this front, Obama has realised that the change of direction must appear to be radical and spectacular. It is therefore indispensable for Washington to adopt unilaterally its own plan to combat global warming, and this plan has to appear strict and ambitious.

The aim is to regain the advantage over the EU by forming alliances with emerging powers while at the same time uniting with the EU to impose on emerging nations a deal favourable to the multinationals of the North. Although the EU may balk at this, it cannot avoid cooperating because it too wants to force the hand of emerging nations and knows it cannot do it without Uncle Sam.[203]

If the aim of this competition between powers were to develop a sustainable energy policy as quickly as possible, there would not be too much harm done. But this is far from being the case. Competition is in all fields, including reducing the price of carbon credits and therefore lengthening the fossil-fuel era. On this subject, Waxman-Markey, with its 'mechanisms of compensation', has gone further than the EU 'climate package', so that it is reasonable to assume that the EU, in the name of competitiveness, will also offer advantageous deals to its industrial sectors. Obama does indeed wish to favour investment in renewables[204] but he knows that their commercial potential cannot satisfy the bulimic greed for energy of the capitalist Moloch. He has therefore four priorities: 'clean coal', biofuels, nuclear power and 'clean cars'. This list should have sufficed to vaccinate anyone with a minimum of social and ecological awareness against Obama-mania but unfortunately this has not been the case. Following the example of the Social Democrats, European Green Parties danced and threw rose petals for Obama's triumphant progress to the White House.

In the next chapter, we shall return to the discussion of a certain number of technological choices. At this stage of the argument, it is important above all to emphasise that these choices result from a decision about the role of American capitalism in global competition, not from a desire to stabilise the climate at the optimum level. This is evident in particular in Obama's arguments in favour of oil and biofuels.

In Obama's plan, we read: 'Coal is our most abundant source of energy and is a decisive component in the economic development of China, India and other emerging nations.' The next sentence is revealing: 'Obama believes that the necessary action against climate change requires us to avoid a new phase of building coal-based power stations. Instead, we should devote all our efforts to the transfer of low-carbon technologies throughout the world'.[205]

It is advisable to read between the lines of this document. 'Avoiding the construction of more convention coal-based power stations' really means 'organising the construction of our power stations using non-conventional coal, with carbon capture'. The choice of coal develops logically from the geo-strategic aim of reducing dependence on imported oil and making the US once more the energy leader of the world. Firstly, the proven reserves of coal should last for 300 years at the current rate of consumption. Most of this coal is located in the US ('the Saudi Arabia of coal'), and coal is a major US export (increasing by 45% in 2008).[206] Secondly, India, China and South Africa also have significant coal deposits, and they fear that they will not be able to continue to use these freely. By selling them technology said to be based on 'clean coal', the US could gain allies in climate negotiations. Thirdly, this 'clean coal' would open a vast field of foreign investment to American capital. Besides reinforcing US imperialism against its competitors, these exports of capital would also allow the creation of the precious cheap credits which the US will need in order to keep polluting up to 2026 and beyond.

Mutatis mutandis, the calculation of Obama follows in the wake of Bush's creation of the 'Asia Pacific Alliance for the Climate', uniting the big coal producers – America, Australia, India and China. It is similar in the field of biofuels. When he was Senator for Illinois (third from the top of American States producing ethanol from corn), Obama did a lot to support this baneful industrial sector, which has experienced a boom thanks to generous incentives offered by the Administration.

When George W Bush announced his decision to increase the amount of compulsory ethanol in petrol from 5 billion to 36 billion gallons by 2022, the planet resounded with protests in the name of the fight against famine, of food price stability and of biodiversity. None of this was aimed against Obama. His announced intention of increasing the ethanol quota of 60 billion gallons by 2030 – to almost double that amount[207] has been met with an astonishing silence. 'Corn ethanol is the greatest success in the field of alternative fuels', Obama claims. And he continues, without fear of demagoguery: 'We must combat the attempts of the oil companies to undermine this nascent industry'.[208]

This glosses over an underlying falsehood! Oil companies and agri-business are up to their necks in the production of biofuels. The multinational BP, now re-named Beyond Petrol, has invested 500 million dollars in the creation of a research institute, Energy Bioscience Institute, whose mission is to mobilise the 'genetic genius for developing third generation biofuels from plants, algae and genetically modified bacteria'.[209] ExxonMobil and Shell have similar projects. Biofuels are in favour with oil companies because they are compatible with their current distribution networks and those of the car industry, because there is no need to modify existing engines.

As for agri-business, it is making an outrageous profit from the promotion of ethanol by the US authorities. In March 2007 the price of a bushel of corn soared to 4.38 dollars thanks not only to speculation in agricultural products, but also because of massive subsidies to farmers, tax concessions to oil refineries and protectionist barriers against importation of Brazilian ethanol.[210] Brazilian ethanol is cheaper because it is a by-product of sugar cane, with a seriously exploited workforce. The 'useful productive life' of sugar-cane workers has dropped to 12 years. At the end of slavery, it was 15 to 20 years.[211]

Faced with this tough competition, Archer Daniels Midland, the top global producer of ethanol, does not rely on 'the invisible hand of the market' but on the support of the state. About 50% of the profits are due to the largesse of the Administration with the taxpayers footing the bill. As long as the price of oil remains high (and it is improbable that it will drop in the long term), profit will continue to soar, encouraging farmers to produce for the oil companies.

The US case is simple because, since George W Bush had got tangled up in an untenable climate policy, a change of direction was necessary, and the supporters of this change, led by Obama, have had to make their strategic project explicit. But it goes without saying that the climate policies of other capitalist nations are similarly conditioned by the specific nature of national economic interests. Thus, the reasons why the EU developed quite early on an energy policy based on diversification of supplies increased energy efficiency, and some promotion of renewables can be traced to the fact that the EU has no significant oil reserves or cheap gas supplies whereas the US has a certain amount of control over the black gold of the Middle East.

Making a virtue of necessity, the European Commission has never concealed that its strategic aim was the eco-industry market. 'Once the Kyoto Protocol is in force, the global market in clean technologies ought to prosper', said a pamphlet issued a few years ago.[212] As at 2002, the market was estimated at 550 billion euros, and experts assessed its potential increase over the next five years, especially in developing countries, at a rate of between 5% and 8%.[213]

With EU businesses leading the renewables sector and dominating the water sector, another promising market within the framework of climate change, the EU is well placed to secure a share of the eco-industry market. On this point the European Commission does not hesitate to rub its hands cynically: 'A great number of anticipatory measures will generate a net profit for the economy, for example, measures aimed at a more efficient use of water in regions which will have to cope with water shortages'.[214] Selling privatised water to people suffering from thirst is indeed an easy way of making money.

We can understand why, far from being weakened by the failure of negotiations in The Hague in November 2000, Brussels stayed the course until the Marrakesh agreements. The EU then launched a Coalition for Renewable Energy — the OPEC of renewables according to Margot Walström, former Environmental Commissioner — comprising about 80 countries.

But competition is also fierce within the EU and every member state has its own interests to promote. France defends AREVA, a nuclear energy consortium, by trying to get nuclear power recognised as a 'low carbon' energy source. Denmark swears by wind turbines from Vestas, the global leader in the sector. Germany is competing with Japan to be the global leader in photovoltaics, and promotes the technology by supporting research and by a price policy very favourable to manufacturers.[215]

What can we expect from the policies? At best, a stabilisation of greenhouse gases in the atmosphere at around 650 ppmCO_2 eq, implying a rise in temperature of between at least 3.2°C and 4°C plus a rise in sea levels of 0.6 and 2.4 metres (without taking into account the break-up of the ice caps).

Appalled at the prospect of planetary chaos, the great powers say they want to come together around a common climate policy. However this is continually undermined and brought down to the lowest common denominator by the mechanisms of competition. As a result we are rapidly being dragged towards a situation even more dangerous than the 'safe-ish' one envisaged by *The Economist*. The strategy appears more ambitious than Kyoto but in particular it is more neo-liberal. Instead of removing inequalities, it makes them worse. Instead of freeing the peoples of the Global South from the imperialist yoke, it makes them more subject to it. Above all it is woefully inadequate from the point of view of reducing emissions! Beyond the soothing rhetoric of politicians, we need to confront the evidence. 'We have our feet glued to the accelerator and are hurtling towards the abyss'. These were not the words of France's Olivier Besancenot[216] or of sub-commandante Marcos of the Zapatistas. They were spoken by Ban Ki-Moon, General Secretary of the United Nations.[217]

Chapter Nine
THE SORCERERS' APPRENTICES

Throughout this book we have taken care not to focus on disaster scenarios. We mistrust gurus who encourage fear in order to draw in their followers. Quite often they throw in some scientific data in order to baffle people, keep them quiet and make them accept the unacceptable. Unfortunately, there is a tendency on the Left to believe in 'salvation through catastrophe', according to Riesel and Semprun.[218] This tendency to adopt the most alarmist prognosis in the hope of galvanising the masses to take to the streets runs the risk that the opposite will occur. Panic is no substitute for understanding and the campaign will not be radicalised in this way.

This is why this book has been based strictly on the diagnostics and projections of the IPCC while at the same time emphasising the major uncertainty concerning the break-up of the ice caps. We have not raised the spectre of a massive and sudden release of methane stocks in the depths of the ocean and we have left to others the task of speculating upon the risk of all this gas flaring up and transforming the planet into a ball of fire.[219] Nevertheless we have reached extremely worrying conclusions because, unless scientists are completely mistaken, the situation is really very alarming. There is a risk that it will become even worse if we take into account the consequences for the poor of the world, and the technological choices by which capitalism tries to reconcile accumulation for profit with climate stabilisation.

Knowing the limits of current policies aimed at mitigating the effects of global warming, we can approach the question of adaptation, that is, the measures needed to help people adapt to the likely consequences of climate change. (We left this to one side in Chapter 5 having mentioned its major importance for the countries of the Global South, in particular for the exploited and oppressed of these countries. Let us now return to the subject.) Adaptation and mitigation are linked because the greater the mitigation the more limited the adaptation can be and vice versa. Since policies of mitigation are inadequate, it would be advisable at the very least to prepare an urgent response to the considerable needs for adaptation in countries with minimal resources where the signs of climate change are already dramatic.

In this field as well, the governments of industrialised countries are cynically refusing to accept their responsibilities. Not content with ignoring the need to take precautions, they are also turning their backs on their own liberal principle that 'the polluter must pay'. According to the United Nations Development Programme (UNDP), adaptation would require the transfer of 86 billion dollars a year from North to South from 2015 onwards.[220]

Until the 2009 Copenhagen climate summit, the funds pledged for adaptation in the course of international discussions amounted to barely 26 million dollars. These funds were intended to come partly from the total resources of the CDM so that the budgets available for adaptation were not determined by the needs of the recipients but by their degree of openness to 'clean' investments by the multinationals. Furthermore, the World Bank and the IMF would hold most of the funds, dispersing them among numerous different accounts which would not be managed by Third World countries.

The difference between the 86 billion dollars required and the 26 million dollars raised could mean that hundreds of millions of people will suffer – principally children, women and the elderly. Even 86 billion dollars represents barely 0.2% of the GDP of developed countries. It hardly amounts to what the UK government spends weekly on the maintenance of flood barriers. And the German State of Baden-Württemberg has a flood-protection budget twice the size of the amounts dedicated to adaptation for the entire Global South.

The injustice was far too flagrant. Some would like to believe that it was rectified at the Copenhagen summit. Indeed, one of the few concrete decisions taken by the 25 signatories to the agreement is based on the transfer of resources to 'developing' countries. The North undertook to pay 10 billion dollars a year to the South between 2010 and 2012 and this sum was to be increased to 100 billion by 2020. The funds were to be used for the development of green technologies, for the fight against deforestation or for adaptation to climate change. The agreement stipulated that the payments should be 'predictable, new and additional' (so they were not to be deducted from development aid, nor fluctuate according to the decisions of the donors or their budget deficits, etc.).

Nevertheless, extreme caution must be exercised while the concrete financial details are not precisely known. A memorandum issued by the

International Institute for Environment and Development (IIED) raises six key questions: whether the funds are new and additional; who makes the decisions; the nature of the monies (grants or loans?); and the reliability of payments and financial channels.[222] The agreement mentions a large variety of sources, both public and private. However, as the IIED observes: 'The inclusion of private sources of finance could completely change the real meaning of the figures. If a billion dollars of public finance is used to divert nine million dollars of direct foreign investment from coal to renewables, will we refer to 'ten billion dollars of climate finance from public and private sources'?

The new and additional nature of the funding in relation to development aid will be much more difficult to establish since the agreement does not give a year as a reference point. It will be particularly difficult to pinpoint in the area of adaptation, since the idea currently covers such a wide field that it is impossible to distinguish between a policy of adaptation and a policy of 'business as usual'. For instance, is the case of the construction of irrigation systems or the choice of drought-resistant plants an 'adaptation' or 'development'?

Clearly the nature of the funding is crucial. Since the developed capitalist countries are responsible for more than 70% of global warming it should be a question of grants. But this is far from being self-evident and some governments – that of the UK in particular – have already decided that the funding will be in the form of loans.

After the final meeting in Copenhagen, the delegate from Tuvalu concluded his contribution by saying, in biblical terms, 'the money offered to us is reminiscent of Judas's Thirty Pieces of Silver'. Indeed! But the climate Judases will have to pay interest to modern-day Pontius Pilates.

Thus, while media reports carry the self-satisfied discourse of politicians who call their *climate packages* or *climate bills* 'historic', the conditions developing behind the scenes are threatening to become a mass crime against hundreds of millions of human beings whose responsibility for the emission of greenhouse gases is negligible – indeed, close to zero.

Polemical exaggeration? No, a sad truth. The basis for a criminal mismanagement of future climate catastrophes is developing before our eyes. Tuvalu, (26 km^2, 11,636 inhabitants) a country 3,400 kilometres northeast of Australia consisting of eight marvellous atolls rising to 4.5 metres above sea-level, already has 3,000 climate refugees. The climate policies of developed countries have very probably condemned it to disappear before the end of the century.

In 2000, when the government of this tiny state requested that Australia and New Zealand take in its citizens in the case of an emergency, Canberra refused. Oozing cynicism, the Minister for Immigration, Peter Ruddock, went so far as to declare that accepting any refugees from Tuvalu would be 'discriminating' against other refugees. 'Australia has slammed the door in our faces' commented a Tuvalu spokesperson. New Zealand agreed to take 74 persons a year on condition that they were aged between 18 and 45, already had an offer of employment 'acceptable' in New Zealand, (salaried, full-time, long-term post), could prove their ability to speak English, could satisfy certain health conditions and had sufficient financial resources to support any dependents.[223] What about the old, the children, the sick – let them drown? 'Out of sight, out of mind' seems to be the attitude to casualties of climate change.

The basic injustice of climate change resides in the fact that it is the workers, the unemployed, the peasant farmers and the urban proletariat of poor countries who are the main victims of a phenomenon caused in large part by capitalist development in the North.[224] At the same time, the capitalist response to climate change threatens the exploited and oppressed everywhere, including in 'rich' countries. Not only do they have to foot the bill for an ineffectual policy, but their very existence may be endangered, as was shown by the example of Hurricane Katrina in New Orleans, in September 2005. We have already discussed the human cost of this catastrophe in Chapter 3. Given the social inequalities that characterise capitalist society, it is evidently no coincidence that African-American women (and their children) paid the highest price.

The Katrina catastrophe is also inseparable from the racist and imperialist class policies of the US bourgeoisie in general, and the Bush Administration in particular. From 2003 onwards, in order to finance the 'war on terror', the US systematically reduced the budget of the department responsible for the maintenance of sea walls. In fact in 2005 this department received barely one-sixth of the funding requested.

Two months before Hurricane Katrina, the Federal Emergency Management Agency (FEMA) released an emergency plan based on the cynical hypothesis that, in the case of flooding, the poor would remain where they were – since they did not have the financial resources to pay for their evacuation. 'The inhabitants must realise that they will be left to their own devices for several days', declared Michael Brown, head of FEMA. In July 2005 the municipal authorities warned the inhabitants that they 'would be largely responsible for their own safety'.[225] This staggering policy of arrogance and brutality, contrary to the basic principle of expecting all states to protect their citizens, was continued after the hurricane. A strategy of reconstruction was aimed at driving the poor from the city and undermining the social gains of the workers, especially by abolishing the minimum wage.[226]

It will be argued that Tuvalu and New Orleans are exceptional cases. This may be true, but predictions of other unpleasant global warming scenarios are springing up like mushrooms even in the *think tanks* of power. In this context, we will recall the apocalyptic report that two self-styled experts produced some time ago for the Pentagon. Announcing a rush of climate refugees, this document predicts that Europe would be submerged, while the US and Australia 'would probably be fortresses, since these countries have the resources and the reserves to allow them to be self-sufficient'. The authors went so far as to claim coldly that, around these fortresses, 'deaths from war as well as starvation and disease will decrease population size, which over time, will re-balance with carrying capacity'.[227]

Hardly anyone has drawn attention to the fact that the scientific value of this so-called study is non-existent. This is first of all because it implicitly agrees with those who claim that climate change is natural in origin. Secondly, following the example of the disaster movie *The Day After Tomorrow*, it postulates that the threat of a new glaciation and of a rise in sea-level can occur at one and the same time. This is absolute nonsense since, if there is more ice at the poles, there is less water in the oceans. But the most worrying aspect of the study is the absence of protest against the ecological concept of 'carrying capacity' which has no relevance for the analysis of social relations between humanity and nature and is used to support a despicable socio-political project – the large-scale extermination of the poor.

Unfortunately, this report is no exception. There is a long list of reactionary fantasies inspired by global warming. Thus, some have raised the question of whether the market for greenhouse gas emission rights should be complemented by a market in 'rights to procreate', with the pretext that the 'population explosion' of developing countries is a major cause of climate destabilisation.

Harsh ideological and social battles are taking place, especially on the subject of population. There was a modest foretaste of this when a current within the most important US organisation for the protection of nature, the Sierra Club, campaigned for the end of immigration to be made a priority 'ecological' demand of their movement.[228] The moles of the Far Right have been unmasked and defeated. Nevertheless, we must continue to exercise extreme vigilance. Indeed, the question of population is entering the climate debate by the front door – the UN – in guises which appear completely above suspicion.

A few weeks after the Copenhagen Summit, the UN Fund for Population Activities (UNFPA) published a report on 'Women, Population and Climate'.[229] In this, we read that climate change negotiations 'would have a better chance of succeeding' if 'population dynamics, relations between the sexes and women's health' were taken into account.[230] The report makes a link between family planning programmes and a reduction in CO_2 emissions. Yet in reality, since demographic changes are extremely slow, it is difficult to see how the programme recommended by the authors could make any significant contribution to reduction of emissions starting in 2015 at the latest, with further reductions of 80% by 2050, and by at least 95% in developed countries – where the population is already starting to decline.

Evidently it cannot be denied that world population has an effect on *future* climate change, but to what extent? Looking at the period 1950 – 1990 we note that the population increase in so-called 'developing' countries contributed significantly less to the rise in CO_2 emissions than the increase in consumption in developed nations and even than the increase in population in the latter. Furthermore, if the countries of the South had kept their population at 1950 levels, while adopting the levels of emission in the countries of the North, global warming would be much worse than at present. On the other hand, if the emissions per inhabitant of the North had been equal to those of the South, global warming would be considerably less than its current level, even in the absence of any population control policies.[231]

Population is a factor to be taken into account,[232] but not as a cause of climate change, still less a solution to the drastic reduction of emissions which must be implemented within a very short space of time. Demographic transition aimed at stemming population growth has to a large extent been initiated in developing countries, where it is progressing faster than had been envisaged. Its continuation is to be welcomed. Such a transition can be achieved above all through social progress, development of good systems of social security, women's education and their right to control their own fertility (including the right to safe abortions). Even so, this is necessarily a long-term strategy.

Short of opting for unheard-of barbarity, no system for reducing population growth offers part of the answer to the ecological emergency. The authors of the report 'Women, Population and Climate' are well aware of this. We cannot therefore avoid asking what their real aims are. In any case it is clear that, under the pretext of improving women's health, the document shows a tendency to reduce the North's responsibility for climate change by adding the population of the South to the equation...

The process is shocking. But this is not all. Cost-efficiency is invoked in the report to give this policy the semblance of a scientific basis. 'According to research by the LSE (London School of Economics), every seven dollars spent on family planning would result in the saving of more than a ton of CO_2 per annum on a global scale. The same saving, obtained via green technologies, would cost 32 dollars'.[233]

The attempt to stabilise the climate with the mechanisms of the market shows its true face here. All things considered, according to this logic of cost, the most economic climate policy would be quite simply to let several hundred million human beings starve to death, as the 'experts' from the Pentagon have implicitly recommended. We will return to this in the next chapter, when we examine the place of the climate crisis in the historical development of capitalist society. Before that, however, we must discuss three technological choices which threaten to aggravate environmental and social impacts and also the risk that 'capitalist climate policy' (if this expression makes any sense!) will career out of control. Truly headlong rushes forward, these choices all develop directly from the fact that the system cannot possibly envisage any reduction of material production, so cannot give up its bulimic consumption of energy.

The first headlong rush into the future involves the massive production of biofuels. This constitutes a remarkable example of capitalism's tendency towards irrationality on a global scale. In fact, the energy balance sheet for biofuel production is negative in every case except that of sugar cane! The carbon balance sheet is therefore negative as well.

According to the Institute of European Environmental Policy, the carbon released from deforestation linked to biofuels could exceed carbon savings by 35% in 2011 rising to 60% in 2018.[234] This indirect impact is not considered in European sustainability guidelines and had not been taken into account when the EU adopted its 'energy and climate package'.

The social and environmental costs of biofuels are very worrying. Although they only cover an infinitesimal fraction of energy needs in the transport sector, ethanol and biodiesel are already showing their harmful effects, to which Jean Ziegler and others have drawn attention.[235]

The logic of production for profit leads to the production of ethanol and biodiesel for those who can pay. Their demands are given priority over the basic human right to food, over the rights of indigenous communities, over health (many populations are threatened by the extensive use of pesticides) and over the protection of the environment. Transition to second-generation biofuels does not in itself eliminate these dangers. Even supposing that there were regulations strict enough to prevent the allocation of agricultural land for the production of cellulose ethanol, the demand from the transport sector is such that it would be necessary to devote enormous tracts of land to monoculture. And that would have many consequences in terms of pollution and destruction of biodiversity.

Locally and on a small scale, production of biofuels from agricultural waste could be a transitional development point for some rural communities. Large-scale production, however, should be forbidden, as it entails not only impoverishment of the soil due to the break-up of the cycle of nutrients, but also unreasonable use of fertiliser, which is harmful to the environment and the climate and requires large amounts of energy to produce.[236]

One point that has not been sufficiently emphasised is that the rush for biofuels (and for the creation of 'carbon sinks') gives a vigorous impetus to genetic technologies, leading to a qualitative increase in the associated risks. Genetically modified trees constitute a subject of major concern. The ninth Conference of the UN Framework Convention on Climate Change (UNFCCC) in Milan 2003, included the planting of these trees as one of the techniques which could confer the right to carbon credit within the framework of the CDM. This decision represents a major concession to various industrial sectors, interested in rapidly growing GM trees (which reduces the time necessary for the production of wood and credits), or in trees containing less lignin (which reduces the cost and the energy necessary for turning the cellulose into ethanol or paper).

However, GM trees constitute several specific risks for the environment and for human health.[237] For instance, there is the risk that pollen from trees genetically modified in order to produce a natural insecticide (Bt) would be particularly harmful to allergy-prone people, because, for several years before being harvested, the trees would produce a great deal of pollen with new allergenic properties. On 31 March 2006, the 8th Conference of the UN Convention on Biodiversity had adopted a declaration formally warning against the use of GM trees but the UNFCCC did not take it into account.[238]

An even more serious threat could be posed by research into the production of third-generation biofuels from bacterial cultures and GM micro-algae. The use of these rapidly multiplying organisms increases the dissemination of genes, since the areas necessary for cultivation would be so huge (sites thousands of hectares in size in tropical countries) that containment would be impossible. It is in this area that the pressure in favour of GM research appears greatest. The new alliances between monopoly capital of the oil sector and agri-business speak for themselves. The Energy Bioscience Institute, to which we have already referred, links the oil multinational BP with the seed company Mendel Biotechnology and thus to Monsanto, world leader in genetic engineering.[239]

The second headlong rush is towards 'clean coal' – carbon capture and storage (CCS). CCS consists of using chemical processes to isolate carbon dioxide produced by large power stations (or to decarbonise it before use) and to place it in a 'supercritical' state (between gas and liquid) in order to inject it into deep geological strata, where it can be stored. CCS has already been implemented on an industrial scale at a certain number of sites, especially in Norway and the US.[240] No problems – so far! According to the IPCC's special report on CCS, 'the net result is that a power station with CCS could reduce CO_2 emissions by 80% - 90%, in comparison to a power station without it'.[241] CCS thus appears to offer at least a partial solution to the problem of the balance between development and the fight against climate change. Nevertheless, certain observations should be made.

Firstly, 'clean coal' is a myth if we take into account the difficulty of extraction, pollution by coal dust, radioactive pollution, consequences for health, destruction of landscapes and the ecological impact of coal-mines. Limited space does not permit us to discuss these problems in detail, but one of the most serious threats is poisoning by heavy metal, in particular mercury. There has been a worrying increase in emissions of mercury as coal regains the upper hand in energy markets and causes serious pollution, not only on a local but on a global scale.[242] Furthermore, with reference to greenhouse gas emissions, CCS does not control everything, since the extraction of a ton of carbon releases on average 13 kg of methane.

Secondly, the long-term safety of storage facilities is evidently a huge problem. Although some gases have remained quietly contained in the depths of the ocean for hundreds of millions of years, complete safety can never be entirely guaranteed. An earthquake could always cause a leakage. In such a case, the sudden release of vast quantities of CO_2 could drastically increase the greenhouse effect. Furthermore, if a weak concentration of carbon dioxide is not dangerous, the same cannot be said of massive amounts. The inhabitants of the shores of Lake Nyos in Cameroon can testify to this.

Nyos is situated in the crater of an extinct volcano and is saturated with CO_2 emanating from a pocket of magma beneath the lake. On 21 August 1986, after a minor earthquake (or renewed volcanic activity – the actual cause was not clear), 1.6 million tonnes of CO_2 were suddenly released into the atmosphere. Aided by the topography of the region, the concentration of CO_2 in the atmosphere exceeded 10%, killing 1,700 people and 3,500 head of cattle within a radius of 25 km.[243] In the case of industrial storage in densely populated regions (such as Silesia, where the EU is funding the

RECOPOL project)[244], an escape of gas could cause serious accidents...

Thirdly, the effects of storage on geological strata are unknown. As incredible as it may seem, some geologists and geo-physicists fear that increased pressure may increase the risk of earthquakes or volcanic eruptions. Far-fetched? Perhaps not. The scientists rely particularly on the fact that the seasonal variations in the amount of ice in the arctic regions influence the frequency of eruptions, because of changes in the underground pressure.[245] Thus, the annual insertion over ten years of a million tons of CO_2 into the saline aquifers of the North Sea could have been the cause of a recent seismic shock measuring 4 on the Richter scale. Had it been more violent it would have caused a tsunami. CCS could therefore pose a danger to future generations in the same way as nuclear waste.

On the other hand, there is no escape from a mortal danger without risk. It is not possible to insist on the one hand on the urgent necessity for a drastic reduction of emissions and on the other hand to refuse on principle to envisage certain solutions for the sole reason that they are not structural, or that their long-term effects are not perfectly understood. We argue that prudent use of CCS under certain conditions would be acceptable, within the framework of a strategy of rapid phasing-out of fossil fuels. This would allow for the retraining of miners, who should not pay the price for energy transition, any more than other workers in polluting industries.

But this is in no way the perspective from which this matter is currently viewed. On the contrary, in the eyes of its promoters CCS appears to be a green light for a new era of coal use lasting several centuries, in other words a new attempt to extend physical limits without worrying about the consequences. And these consequences are not only long-term. Within a very short time, the rush to use coal promises to extend the list of what Isabelle Stengers and Philippe Pignarre call 'infernal alternatives'.[246] The alternative 'water or energy', for instance, should be taken into consideration, because washing coal requires enormous quantities of water, as do other technologies, such as the transport of coal in liquid form as 'carboduc' or the synthesis of liquid fuel from coal, as a replacement for oil.[247]

Last but not least – the fourth and most dangerous headlong rush is obviously the development of nuclear energy. Once the enthusiasts for nuclear power were the most vociferous among the ranks of climate sceptics. Now they have realised how to use global warming to their advantage. From now on, they are presenting their technological fetish as the *deus ex machina* which alone can save humanity from the apocalypse.

We shall not devote much space here to discussion of radioactive waste, or the risk of accidents (recently highlighted by the Fukushima catastrophe), nor deal with the threat posed by close co-operation between civil and military nuclear research. These are very important questions – in fact, nuclear power is still by far the greatest technological threat, and probably the only possible future cause of humanity's total self-destruction. But the arguments on this subject are fairly well known and have been widely discussed since Fukushima.[248] Within the framework of this book it would seem more worthwhile to emphasise the absurdity of the use of atomic energy among the panoply of tools to use against the climate tipping-point.

First of all, CO_2-free atomic energy is a delusion. Studies have even shown that if the chain of production of nuclear energy is taken into account – from the manufacture of the fuel to the decommissioning of power stations and waste disposal – this sector emits more CO_2 per kWh than a co-generation gas power station and about a third of the emissions of a high-performance gas power station.[249]

More fundamentally, we cannot avoid agreeing with the argument developed by Benjamin Dessus and Hélène Gassin[250] that nuclear energy would not be able to meet the peak demand for electricity because it functions on a quasi-continuous basis. At best it could only replace two-thirds of the production of fossil fuel power stations, thus reducing by 30% emissions linked to energy production (and about 15% of total emissions). This is not only far from the 85% deemed necessary as a precaution, it also appears in practice to be completely unattainable.

The roughly 400 nuclear power stations existing globally hardly meet 17% of electricity needs. In the light of the knowledge that the International Energy Agency (IEA) is expecting demand to double between now and 2030, achieving the goal of having two-thirds of electricity requirements generated by nuclear power would mean having to build one new power station a day, whereas construction usually takes about ten years. Once this expensive Herculean task has been completed, it should be acknowledged a that the result had not been worth the effort, because nuclear power can only produce electricity, and electricity only covers 16.2% of global energy needs.

A climate strategy based on atomic energy would need to increase this output to 60% or 70%, which would mean the building of even more power stations and the construction of related networks. It would then still be necessary to have the right fuel and here too there is a problem as known resources of uranium would only be available for 60 years for the current number of power stations.[251]

We must bow to the evidence that atomic energy simply cannot form the axis of a strategy because this axis must be formed by the long-term solution which only renewables can offer. Decisively, renewable energy sources and nuclear energy obey two completely different and opposing strategies for implementation – decentralisation and maximum efficiency in the case of renewables, ultra-centralisation and waste in the case of nuclear power. To opt for a mixture of solar and atomic energy, even in a period of transition, is to try to marry fire and water. In the final analysis this could only complicate the necessary and inevitable energy revolution.

With the exception of certain local applications of biofuels and a moderate use of CCS to facilitate transition, especially at a social level, it would seem that each of these technological headlong rushes, considered separately, should be ruled out.

The 'Blue Map' scenario drafted by the IEA that envisages a 50% reduction of emissions by 2050[252] is probably insufficient as argued above. Not only that, but the list of measures proposed implies the construction every year, for more than 40 years, of 32 nuclear power stations each with a capacity of 1,000 MW, as well as 45 new coal-fired power stations of 500 MW capacity equipped with CCS.

In another context, this proposal by technocrats of a technologically impossible solution might seem rather an amusing paradox. However, especially after Fukushima, no one is laughing any more – the IEA's plan is simply criminal. The dogmatic refusal to reduce energy consumption, share resources and decrease material consumption is the reason and it leads absolutely nowhere. This nonsense is taking place before our very eyes as hundreds of thousands of competing capitalists greedy for energy employ cohorts of high-level experts enclosed in their domains of ultra-specialist competence.

It requires a great deal of optimism, cynicism or recklessness to believe in the birth of a 'green capitalism' or in the 'Green New Deal' proposed by some green parties. Nonetheless, the final chapter will examine whether a change of course worthy of the name is possible within the framework of the system. The question is especially important because the abolition of capitalism does not seem to be on the agenda in the near future...we shall venture into the Holy of Holies of capitalism and try to find out to what extent are the exigencies of ecology compatible with the fundamental law of capitalism – the law of labour-value?

Chapter Ten
THE DESTRUCTIVE DYNAMIC OF CAPITALISM

The current situation appears at first glance to be completely irrational. The climate tipping-point has been perfectly well documented with the exception of the theories of a few sceptics which have been demolished – indeed held up to ridicule.[253]

The scientific community has sounded the alarm. The very probable social and economic consequences of climate change are very well-known. No one can be unaware of the fact that, even though the poor will be most affected, no one will be spared. We know what ought to be done and that the technological solutions exist. In view of all this, how can we believe that the authorities will put 'their feet on the accelerator', as Ban Ki Moon put it? How can we explain the contradiction that although we live in a society in which the elites claim to govern according to 'reason', even in the most obscurantist periods of its history, humanity has certainly never have known such completely monstrous irrationality.

Given this critical situation one would think it would suffice to explain the basis of the problem for our leaders to radically change their policies. But this is a fiction. Stupidity, greed, ignorance of the facts and 'short-termism' are certainly all factors playing a role to a greater or lesser extent. Yet such a flagrant and persistent irrationality must have structural roots to be found within the laws of society. In the course of the preceding chapters, we identified three of these laws: production for profit, accumulation and competition between capitals (which is also expressed as rivalry between states). These are evidently linked together and reflect even more profoundly the basic nature of capitalism as a mode of production governed by the law of value. The discussion will be continued at this level.

According to Marx, value exists in the two opposing categories of exchange-value and use-value. Use-value is characterised by its quality of satisfying human needs, while exchange-value is characterised by the amount of human labour it represents. Capitalism is defined as a society of generalised production of exchange-values, in other words of goods.

By definition, these are comparable only in relation to the amount of human labour necessary to produce them, which means that this mode of production reduces all specific and concrete labours to their common denominator of expenditure of calories – of human labour in the abstract.

This abstraction, pushed to its extreme limits by capitalism, expresses itself in money as a representation of exchange value in general, which Marx calls simply 'value'. Under this mode of production, value is thus the aim and the measure of everything. We shall see that the irrationality of capitalist climate policy ensues precisely from this law so that, in the final analysis, reason can only take command with a radical change of paradigm.

With climate policy, the law of value is expressed in the first instance in the fact that cost-efficiency is set up as the supreme criterion of rationality and relevance at every level, from global positioning to the choice of the specific technologies to be implemented in each case. Faced with capitalism, any criticism has been blunted to the extent that observers and experts on climate research consider the pre-eminence of cost-efficiency as self-evident, as if cost-efficiency were a particular application of a natural law. In fact, it is obviously nothing of the sort, since the cost (or the price) of an item of merchandise is not a natural characteristic of the item but the expression of a social relation of production and thus of social contradictions.

Other things being equal, increasing cost-efficiency implies replacing human labour with machines; reducing the value of the workforce (by a rise in the rate of exploitation and/or a reduction of the cost of goods necessary for the maintenance of the workforce); appropriating natural resources to sell them at monopoly prices (although, since they are not the products of labour, they have no exchange-value); or by a combination of all of the above. None of these measures have anything 'natural' about them.

Consequently, maximising the cost-efficiency of climate policy will require a change in the relationship of forces between different classes of society and affect access to natural resources to the detriment of the exploited. This is what Nicholas Stern refers to in his report when emphasising the importance of raising public awareness. He says: 'Continued pressure from the public in favour of action against climate change gives politicians the courage to take measures which they might otherwise have considered too risky or unpopular'.[254]

Apart from the fact that cost-efficiency leads to shameful social strategies, the basic problem is that cost-efficiency is an inadequate criterion of ecological rationality for climate policy. As a purely quantitative indicator, value is by definition incapable of integrating the qualitative elements indispensable for energy transition. This congenital flaw is especially obvious in the way the rights market operates. While elimination of fossil carbon emissions implies the radical reduction and ultimate abandonment of the use of fossil fuels, it is not merely a question of quantities but also of achieving qualitative change. We need an energy revolution which implies a controlled use of natural resources together with a reorganisation of society. And this means a strategic plan centred on numerous qualitative and quantitative elements, both in the ecological and social sphere.

Let us take an example. In view of the urgency of the situation, we cannot exclude the recourse under certain conditions to non-structural solutions such as the planting of trees to absorb carbon. But a tonne of CO_2 absorbed by a forest, a tonne of CO_2 not emitted thanks to thermal insulation of a house and a tonne of CO_2 not emitted thanks to the use of photovoltaic panels do not have the same ecological significance. The first is the result of a temporary measure which gains time without resolving any structural problems. The second is the result of a structural measure consistent with the axis of the energy revolution. The third is the result of an investment which, as we have seen, would only be rational within the framework of a reduction of energy needs – a *sine qua non* for the replacement of fossil fuels by renewables, instead of using them side by side.[255]

The market simply cannot take into account these differences in quality, decisive for the development of a coherent climate policy. The reason for this is the very nature of value. As goods, two permits to emit a tonne of CO_2 are only distinguished by their cost, thus by the amount of human labour they represent, with no sign of the quality of the processes which generated them.

The actual labour needed to plant trees in the Third World is very much less complex than the numerous operations needed to replace thermal power stations by decentralised and low-cost solar power stations and the cost of the labour force in the first case is significantly lower than in the second. So the criterion of cost-efficiency automatically directs the economy to non-structural measures, which produce cheap emission rights, rather than towards the indispensable energy revolution.

In other words, instead of favouring a controlled transition towards a new energy system, and organising this system according to a short, medium and long-term vision, the law of value blindly spurs a febrile rush towards the cheapest emission rights. These rights are also the least relevant from the point of view of ecological quality (and, as we have seen, threaten to lead to barbaric population policies). We could denounce the stupidity of offset mechanisms, but they are consistent with the basic law of capitalism, the law of value, and this consistency supports their legitimacy. It is in fact the law of value itself that should be called into question as the basis of the economy. Climate change has shown us how inadequate it is for even identifying real human needs, let alone satisfying them.

The same reasoning applies to the consideration of social impacts. As we have seen, the market in emission rights reduces the quantities of different greenhouse gases to their 'CO_2 equivalent', that is, to the volume of CO_2 which has the same radiative power. Applying this rule to the letter means that vastly different activities can be considered equivalent – such as rice growing (source of methane), itinerant slash-and-burn agriculture (source of non-fossil CO_2) and motor racing (source of fossil CO_2). This list clearly demonstrates that the need to reduce all greenhouse gases to their common characteristic – their radiative power – in order to make them interchangeable is only a particular expression of the law of value, which reduces all concrete human labour to the common abstract characteristic of expenditure of energy.

Obviously, from a social point of view, it is by no means immaterial whether rice production is curtailed, or indigenous peoples are prevented from pursuing their traditional way of life, or we have to say goodbye to the Monaco Grand Prix. However, of all these choices, the most 'efficient' would be to expropriate the indigenous inhabitants of the forest and prevent them from continuing their way of life. Since these societies are not subject to the law of value their destruction would not harm any balance sheets. On the contrary, the appropriation of their forest resources would allow the sale of carbon credits.

Thus the communities whose experience and vision of the world could help modern society to develop a mode of production in harmony with nature would be wiped out by capitalism, in the name of the defence of that same nature. This is a good example of something Marx often denounced – the logic of the market that causes reality to be perceived upside-down.

In fact, the most efficient way to radically reduce the emissions while bearing in mind the qualitative imperatives of transition would be not to use fossil fuels more than is compatible with the stabilisation of the climate at the highest possible level. This limit has been determined with a fair degree of precision by researchers at the Potsdam Institute for Climate Research.[256]

In 2011 the global economy had already used a third of the carbon budget of 886 gigatonnes of carbonic gas ($GtCO_2$) available for the period 2000 – 2050. The available balance is only 565 $GtCO_2$. The proven reserves of fossil fuels in the hands of public companies, private companies and governments correspond to the emission of 2,795 $GtCO_2$. Reserves controlled by the ten largest private companies in the coal, gas and oil sectors correspond to 745

$GtCO_2$ while the rest is controlled by states, especially Saudi Arabia.

The fact that the amount of fossil carbon available is only 565 of a total of 2,795 GtC02 implies that, in order not to damage the climate too much, 80% of the known reserves of coal, oil and gas should remain in the ground and never be burnt. These reserves, counted as assets by their owners, contribute to decisions about the course of action of the businesses concerned. Thus, as Duncan Clark wrote in the *Guardian*, 'If the greater part of the reserves of oil, coal and gas may not be consumed, the primary assets of the largest energy companies in the world could be as toxic as the thorny security debts which led to the financial collapse of 2008'.[257]

In comparison with this carbon bubble, the property bubble which caused the failure of Lehman Brothers in 2008 appears almost a joke, because the companies concerned Shell, BP, Exxon, for example are the pillars of global capitalism. More powerful than governments, they will do anything and everything to prevent the destruction of their capital. Planned investments testify to this, in particular, that of Glencore which has carried out the most significant capital investment by a giant multinational on the London market. As for Shell, over four years it will invest £62 billion in order to produce 3.7 million barrels of oil a day by 2014, an increase of 12% over 2010.

In this race to invest, the banks, pension funds and hedge funds will support the multinationals of the energy sector because what they do figures prominently in their portfolios. Furthermore, it is finance capital that advances the multinationals the enormous sums of money needed for large long-term fixed capital investments (particularly great in the energy sector with its refineries, power stations, offshore platforms, etc).

If by 'green capitalism' we understand a system in which the qualitative, social and ecological parameters are taken in account by the numerous competing capital, that is to say even within economic activity as an endogenous mechanism, then we are completely deluded. In fact, we would be talking about a form of capitalism in which the law of value was no longer in operation, which is a contradiction in terms. To imagine that a mode of production based on this law could cease to exploit natural resources is as absurd as to imagine that it could cease to exploit the labour force.

Furthermore, apart from its use in a historically determined context, the labour force is nothing more than one of several natural resources. It expresses the capacity of a human being to function as an energy converter and, from this point of view, there is more than one analogy between the destruction of nature and the exploitation of the workforce by capital. It is an identical process.[259]

Consequently, the only question worth discussing is whether the spontaneous destructive dynamic of capitalism can be corrected by a mechanism that, strictly speaking, stands outside the economic sphere. In other words can the law of value be partly neutralised on a long-term basis by decisions taken in the political sphere. We shall examine this question strategically, in terms of what tools to use, and by examining the structural obstacles posed by contemporary capitalism.

From the strategic point of view, the analogy between exploitation of the workforce and exploitation of natural resources prompts an examination of the problem in the light of the actions of workers over the past century. A substantial part of this action, in the trade union, mutualist and cooperative sectors at any rate, has consisted of attempts to limit the scope of the law of value. Thus, collective negotiations of labour contracts and the introduction of a system of social security limits the damage by preventing to some extent the purchase, re-sale and discarding of each individual member of the workforce like a piece of merchandise.

At the same time, the fact that the public sector operates in fields such as transport, education, health, etc. implies that these sectors are to some extent protected from the direct effects of the law of value. This is why the workers' movement is justified in defending the public sector, even if much of it was created by capitalism to serve its own interests at a given moment.

The balance sheet of this experience of more than a century of campaigning for solidarity and common ownership is far from negative – there have been some real gains. On the one hand, however, these gains have been due to mass struggle, demonstrations and strikes, including general strikes and sometimes severely repressed revolutions. On the other hand, these gains are constantly under attack by the system. These have been relentless for the last 30 years, and one only has to glance at the newspapers to realise that attacks have intensified since the recession of 2008.

Supporters of 'green capitalism' have nothing in common with the workers who have stepped forward to organise the fight against exploitation, often in peril of their lives. The proponents of 'green capitalism' do not rely on social mobilisation or on confrontation with capital, but on lobbying within the dominant social class and on participating in government. Nevertheless, the comparison with the workers' movement remains pertinent since this strategy, *mutatis mutandis*, is that of the right-wing social democracy. There is furthermore a willingness to believe that capitalism can meet ecological challenges, rather like the social democrats of the previous century wanted to believe that capitalism could meet social challenges.

The common idea of these two currents is that the system is changing.

It is in the process of resolving its contradictions – or is capable of doing so – provided it is suitably guided and advised on what tools to use. Even if this mode of production does not resolve its contradictions, it does change and these changes necessitate new strategies, new systems, new theoretical elaborations and ideological justifications. The social-democratic theoreticians of the 'mixed economy' of the past and those backing today's 'green capitalism' or 'Green (New) Deal' have a lot in common. They imagine being able to transform the system, indeed, to modify the course of history. In reality, the system is using them to change its form without changing its nature. This illusion derives from the fact that the more capitalism is socialised, the greater its need of the state, so that private interests seem to recede behind the general interest.

This is nothing new. In his analysis of the effect of the growing concentration of capital, Marx stated:

> Capital directly takes the form of social capital (capital of directly associated individuals), as opposed to private capital, and its enterprises present themselves as social enterprises, as opposed to private enterprises...This is the negation of the capitalist mode of production from the very heart of the system, and consequently a contradiction which abolishes itself and which, at first glance, seems to represent a simple moment of transition towards a new mode of production. It is under this contradictory aspect that the Limited Company makes its appearance. In certain spheres, it re-establishes monopoly and in fact encourages state intervention.[260]

This need for state intervention was in the past the basis for social democratic illusion. Today, it is the basis of the illusion that 'green capitalism' is able to meet the challenge of the ecological and climate crisis.

But what type of state intervention are we talking about here? If we look into the tools proposed for the 'greening' of capitalism, we will discover a flagrant contradiction. While the responsibility of the market is blindingly obvious and while the situation manifestly requires public initiatives, public enterprises, nationalisation by expropriation and public planning, these instruments are in very short supply, if not totally absent. The principal – if not the only – instrument is a market mechanism – the 'internalisation of externalities'. Ask economists how to avoid the catastrophe and there are very few who will suggest taking energy into public ownership. Most will recommend imposing a carbon price determined (but not too closely) with reference to the estimated damage of global warming.[261] This argument is similar to that drummed into society over the past thirty years: too low a carbon price is responsible for global warming, just as too high a price for labour is responsible for unemployment.

To judge by the effectiveness of employment policies based on this principle, we're not out of the woods yet. In fact, as we have seen, the mountain of high prices for carbon has laboured and produced a very small mouse, one too small to discourage the polluters (if they pay the price), but big enough to annoy those impoverished by neo-liberalism. The impracticality of this policy should be obvious but people's thoughts have been so conditioned by the law of value and the general venality it engenders that they cannot imagine any way of solving the problem other than betting on the price of the triggering factor.[262]

From the structural point of view, the way in which the law of value operates today constitutes a huge obstacle. We shall rely here on the ideas developed by Ernest Mandel in *Late Capitalism*. The author begins by reminding the readers that in capitalism, the law of value no longer operates directly via exchange value, as was the case under simple market production, but by average rate of profit:

'The regulatory mechanism is the equalisation of profit rates, that is to say, capitalist competition. Profit is not shared out among competing capitalists in proportion to the surplus value produced by each variable capital investment, but in proportion to the total mass of capital used by each individual firm. Capital which increases the average social productivity of labour by using a larger number of machines can thus appropriate part of the surplus value produced by 'less successful' capitalists (from the point of view of the social productivity of labour). Capital flows from the sectors where the rate of profit is lower than the average to those where it is higher than the average.'

In his examination of the impact of the formation of huge monopoly capitalist organisations on post-war capitalism, Mandel notes: 'The function of these organisations is to make more difficult the ebb and flow of capital in certain sectors of production in order to prevent the equalisation of profit rates (or to postpone it to a later date)'; in other words, 'to consolidate excess profits for a prolonged period'. He concludes: 'The enormous size of some of these conglomerates constitutes a formidable barrier to the penetration of other capital enterprises ... and thus considerably extends the existence of the surplus profits of monopolies.[263]

This phenomenon is decisive for an understanding of the stalemate of capitalist economic policy. Steel, petrochemicals, glass, cement, electricity – all these industries which emit large amounts of CO_2 – are dominated by huge multinationals which soak up part of the surplus value produced by other sectors and thus continue to attract capital in search of surplus profit.

For this situation to change and for investments to be definitively turned away from the polluters, there would need to be political decisions to suspend the mechanisms which generate surplus profits in order to redistribute resources in favour of non-polluting sectors. But the powerful polluters invoke the sacrosanct law of cost-efficiency, which only an anti-capitalist government could oppose, for the simple reason that this law is embedded in the heart of the system.

Within this general framework the fossil fuel sector has a special characteristic which further reinforces the mechanism. Monopolies in this sector have established themselves via the concentration of huge amounts of capital, as well as via private ownership of land and monopolistic appropriation of oil, gas and coal, natural resources present in limited quantities in the sub-soil. Because of this they are in a position to stabilise their excess profits, extend them over longer periods and even to institutionalise them in the form of revenue.

We saw above that oil revenue alone can be estimated at 1,300 billion euros per annum.[264] If we also take into consideration closely related sectors like the automobile industry, the chemical and petro-chemical industries, aeronautics, naval construction, we can understand what enormous pressure is applied to governments, imposing a rhythm and form of climate policy subordinated to the maintenance of its own interests. The rigidity of the energy system is often mentioned. This does not result merely from the life-span of investments (30 – 40 years for a power station), but also, and especially, from the fact that the powerful lobbies cling on to the goose that lays the golden eggs and continually create new 'needs' which justify forcing it to increase its output.

We must emphasise that the formidable ascendancy of the energy lobbies is based on private ownership of land and of finite resources which can be appropriated. The mechanism is that described by Marx in his analysis of capitalist land rent. The monopoly that a small section of the dominant class exercises over the resource allows the price of the least productive deposit to be imposed as the average price in the sector, so that the more productive deposits produce a profit in excess of the average profit. The progressive exhaustion of fossil fuel resources threatens this advantage, but it is illusory to believe that the rise in price of peak oil or gas will put an end to the energy lobbies.

Firstly, known resources of coal are quite sufficient to take over from other energy forces for a long period. Furthermore, the rise in price of 'black gold' makes it worthwhile to exploit less conventional oil resources

– heavy crude oil, tar sands and oil shale – which are extremely destructive ecologically. Finally, the fossil fuel sector ultimately retains the option of postponing financial deadlines by cutting back its enormous revenue so as to remain competitive against renewables, while continuing to earn a more than average profit.[265]

Travis Bradford would have us believe that photovoltaics will supplant oil as easily as mobile phones have supplanted landlines, ushering in the solar era. This is a flight of fancy, as the scenario does not take into account the capacity for interference of the energy sector monopolies. The movements of capital during the rise in oil prices of 2007 – 2008 are instructive. The price of 147 dollars a barrel certainly gave a little help to renewables, but above all, it boosted the exploitation of tar sands in Alberta, Canada, which would cease to be profitable if the price of 'black gold' collapsed. During 2007 and the first three quarters of 2008, the price rise engendered massive profits. During President Bush's two terms of office, the accumulated profits of the 'five sisters' – BP, Chevron, Conoco Phillips, ExxonMobil and Shell – reached the tidy sum of 656 billion dollars. Do you think that this money was heavily invested in renewables? By no means! The oil companies do all they can to adopt an 'eco-look' but their green investments account for barely 4% of their profits,[266] just enough to keep their hand in, no more.

And that is not all. In future the high prices of oil and gas will give priority to technologies enabling the maintenance of profit via a monopolistic appropriation of land. This will be shown, among other things, by absurd choices in the use of green energy – so much so that the expression 'renewable energy sources' will soon seem almost as meaningless as 'sustainable development'.

The case of biofuels is clear. The sudden enthusiasm for this technology does not come out of the blue for exploiting solar radiation converted into chemical energy via biomass guarantees that this energy resource can be appropriated and monopolised via private ownership of land. This explains the massive purchases of land in some tropical countries, mainly by the Gulf States and the energy lobbies.[267]

Similarly, the DESERTEC project represents an attempt to appropriate solar radiation directly via the construction of an ultra-centralised infrastructure, the huge price of which will enable an effective monopoly over the resource and thus an excess profit. The same factors which led to Becquerel's discoveries and to Bouchot's proposals being ignored will continue to have the same effects. Nature itself seems to want to use climate change to make us understand. If there were finally to be an end to fossil fuels, capitalist accumulation would transform entire regions into ecological deserts by planting enormous monocultures producing biofuel. It would destroy the countryside by installing vast quantities of wind-turbines at the expense not only of the land but of its inhabitants.

A recent study by WWF-France clearly demonstrates that the capitalist 'virtuous circle' supposed to extricate us both from the climate crisis and the social crisis only exists in the imagination of its creators. According to this study, a 30% reduction of emissions between now and 2020 would allow the creation of 684,000 jobs in France.[268] This scenario seems even more attractive since it allows us to dispense with nuclear power and with geological storage of CO_2. However, this will not solve the social crisis. The authors of the report admit that: 'This will only apply if there is massive unemployment in 2020. In the contrary case, the demand for labour will bring about a rise in wages, reducing the positive effect on employment'.

Nor will there be any change in the North's domination of the South, as the study does not integrate the export of unemployment to countries which produce fossil fuels: 'In our country, we can assume that the employment potential of electricity from renewables is greater than that of electricity from fossil fuels because the latter is produced with the aid of imported fuels'.

This is 'Made in France' with a green coating.[269] Can it at least extricate us from the climate crisis? Not really, as the authors do not take into account the effect of growth on the level of emissions. Now, even if the energy package were to contain progressively more renewables, the increase in production and consumption, as we have already seen, inevitably implies increased combustion of fossil fuels, especially at the beginning. Since the corresponding emissions have to be deducted from the 30% reduction, we will be a long way from the necessary 40% by 2020.

Let us take another example. In order to combine a radical reduction of global emissions ('contraction') with an equalisation of emissions per individual ('convergence'), and to enable development in the South to catch up with the North with the aid of clean technologies, the late Anil Agarwal[270] proposed that interchangeable emission rights should be distributed to developing countries who are below the per capita quota which the terrestrial ecosystem can support.[271] Countries of the North which failed to reduce their emissions would have to buy these rights. The income from this would allow the countries of the South to obtain the technologies needed for carbon-free development.

We cannot but applaud the idea of equal human rights to the atmosphere and to resources in general, but how would this equality be realised by distributing interchangeable property rights to the governments of the South? Supposing that it were feasible, in the vast majority of cases the operation would do no more than shift the balance in favour of the capitalists of the South. Like their counterparts in the North, they care not a whit for social equality or the environment. The logic of accumulation would not be called into question.

In any case, this project reveals a political fiction. Capitalism in the North is based on the appropriation of natural resources: wood, water, earth, sub-soil. The dominant capitalist groups, historically based in developed countries, will never accept any proposal for their governments to distribute to their competitors in the 'subject' countries an enormous amount of semi-permanent property rights over the atmosphere, which business in the North would then be obliged to purchase.[272] On the contrary, their logic is to profit from catastrophes in the South to increase their stranglehold on the resources of the planet and to extend it to new domains.

In this respect, the market in emission rights represents a new stage the appropriation of the carbon cycle and, beyond that, the atmosphere itself. The market is not a technical tool to be turned on at will to conduct any kind of social or ecological policy. Goods and price comparisons in the market are the product of specific social relations, which are expressed also in the form of the domination of some states by others. Claude Serfati and François Chesnais are right to insist that there is more than a contradiction between capitalism and nature, between the law of value and the need to save the climate; there is antagonism.[273] The violence of this antagonism is expressed in the terrible projections of the social and ecological impacts of global warming.

Capitalism does not encourage green shoots, but decay. So what is the place of climate change in the history of capitalist development? How does this phenomenon relate to the current social and economic crisis, considered by some to be the most serious since 1929?

One way of approaching the question is to examine the graphs of carbon emissions in the various regions of the developed capitalist world since the end of the 19th century.[274] The graph for Western Europe is particularly informative. Two periods of increase, separated by two plateaux, can be identified – from the beginning of the 19th century to the 1920s, and, especially, from the 1950s to the end of the 1960s. This phasing is remarkably consistent with what Ernest Mandel called the 'long waves' of capitalist development.[275] These are epochs of history, more or less extended, during which capitalism tends towards more expansion (such as the 30-year long post-war boom in France), or stagnation (the 1930s) according to the rate of profit.

Mandel based his analysis on the work of Nikolai Kondratieff, but disagreed with him on one decisive point. Unlike the Russian economist, Mandel posited that, if the passage from a long wave of expansion to a long wave of recession is automatic, the reverse process, on the contrary, requires a series of shocks from outside the economic sphere. Thus, according to Mandel, the post-war turning point was made possible by the crushing of the working-class movement under the iron heel of fascist regimes, the drastic increase in the rate of exploitation in other capitalist countries, and enormous public investments which generated deficit and permanent inflation.

If this interpretation is correct, the downside of the miracle of the post-war boom was an unprecedented crash, millions of deaths, terrible destruction and an ocean of debts. In the light of this analysis, Mandel was sceptical as to the possibility of a long wave of expansion beginning in the 1990s. He thought that the recovery of the rate of profit in the previous decade had been insufficient. As for massive unemployment, austerity and the decline of the working-class movement, these were far from constituting 'external shocks' on the scale necessary for a capitalist system suffering more and more from its own laws.

This last point is crucial. Mandel drew particular attention to the growing contradiction between the tendency of the system to increase the exploitation of wage-earners (to offset the tendency for the rate of profit to decrease), on the one hand, and on the other hand the need to achieve surplus value, crystallised in the ever-increasing quantities of products. 'Who is going to pay for all these goods made with machines bought on credit?' he asked. According to Mandel, the problem was bound to become more difficult as time went on. He saw in it a demonstration of the historic exhaustion of this mode of production (the source of his concept of 'late capitalism') and also a threat to civilisation.

Mandel's idea has been validated, though in an unexpected way, by the circumstances of the last 25 years. As economist Michel Husson has demonstrated, the recession started by the *sub-prime mortgage* affair has occurred at the end of a quarter-century with special features, in the course of which the rate of profit increased spectacularly while the rate of accumulation sank.[276]

This strange situation never existed during earlier 'long waves' with high rates of profit (1848-1873, 1983-1913, 1940/47-1967).[277] In all these cases, there was a considerable expansion of productive investments, social progress (relative and in no way automatic, but undeniable), and a certain reduction of inequalities. Today, and for the past 25 years, the reverse is the case. Profits are soaring but remaining in the financial sector, the rate of return demanded on investments implies a frenzied increase in the rate of exploitation, inequalities are spiralling out of control and the cycle is completed by consumption of luxury goods and by debt.[278]

Thus, in evaluating both the socio-economic aspect and the environmental aspect of the situation, we note two new things; an economic period without precedent in the history of capitalism, and an ecological emergency without precedent in the history of humanity. The combination of these two factors is decisive. In my opinion, it rules out any hope that a solution to the crisis worthy of the name could take place without a profound challenge of capitalist taboos.

Coming after 25 years of neo-liberal 'recovery', the 2009 recession shows that the system has not extricated itself its mass of contradictions. On the contrary it is stuck fast, and the stalemate is profound and structural. We fall back willy-nilly on Mandel's central conclusion – that for 'late capitalism' to start again, there would need to be a series of severe 'external shocks'. This would not necessarily be something even worse than Nazism, Fascism and the Second World War. A collapse of energy prices due to a technological breakthrough could do it. But it is precisely this scenario that is unlikely to materialise in the foreseeable future: an increase in the price of resources is more likely to be the order of the day.

On the other hand, let us suppose for a moment that the vast amounts of speculative capital which swell the 'financial bubble' were to flow into the 'real economy' on a long-term basis, feeding a new period of 20-30 years of strong growth. In this case, consumption of fossil fuel would greatly increase (at least for the first 10 years) and greenhouse gas emissions would therefore also increase. In view of the fact that we are already flirting with the point of no return, it is more than probable that the climate tipping point would be hastened. To achieve any other outcome, it would be necessary for capitalism to reconcile a rise in the rate of profit, economic expansion and radical elimination of fossil fuels...but fossil fuels are cheaper than renewables and will remain so for roughly 20 years. In my opinion, this scenario is impossible.

So why do we need to wait? M Pavan Sukhdev, economist and banker with the Deutsche Bank, chosen by the UN Environment Programme to lead a study on re-directing the global economy towards a 'green' model, gives a precious insight: 'The current model has reached its extreme limits, both for the improvement of conditions of life for the poorest, and for the ecological impact that we can impose on the planet – but my clients will only invest if there is a promise of profit, and this is not going to change'.[279]

This says it all. The system has reached its social and environmental limits but will ignore them, and has already started to ignore them, because capitalists will only invest if there is a promise of profit, and profit requires growth. In other words, the growth of productive forces has become the growth of 'destructive forces',[280] not only because more and more socially and environmentally destructive technologies are deployed, but because global capitalism recognises no limits. The law of value makes it structurally impossible for them to be recognised.

Belgian philosopher Isabelle Sengers was correct to write that 'we live in a time of catastrophes'.[281] It now remains to define the outlines of the catastrophe, the tribute paid by the victims and the way it can be paid off. To answer these questions, we need to leave the strictly economic sphere to examine capitalism from a wider perspective as a mode of human development, especially from the point of view of demographics.

Every mode of production is characterised by a specific law of population. Capitalism's law of population demands a 'permanent reserve army of labour' which can be recruited above all from peasant populations adversely affected by agri-business. We will concentrate on this as it is the best illustration of the lethal process in which we are engaged.

Capitalism has introduced a qualitative change in the agricultural sector. Under previous modes of production at a certain stage of development, a relative increase in population encouraged an increase in the productivity of labour. Because there were more mouths to feed people started to clear large areas of forest, until the limits of this process stimulated the invention of intensive practices allowing more production per hectare. Fear of scarcity and famine spurred the increase in productivity.

Under capitalism, the situation is reversed. It is no longer an increase in population that stimulates intensification of agriculture but intensification of agriculture that stimulates an increase in population. The vast majority of the billions of human beings suffering from famine today are in rural areas, and could be perfectly capable of meeting their own needs and those of their families. The two factors which prevent this are that they have no access to land and that they are crushed by competition from agri-business. The ratio of productivity between a poor peasant from the South, who has no beast of burden, does not use fertilizer and has only rudimentary tools, and the huge mechanised concerns of North America, Europe and Argentina, is 1:300, or even 1:500.[282]

On the world market liberalised by the WTO, there is no contest. Dozens of millions in the South go bankrupt every year and it is doubtful whether capitalism in crisis can turn all of these into members of the proletariat. So the question arises, what will happen to all these 'surplus people', trapped between the effects of global warming and the historic exhaustion of the system? Are they not destined to become the 'expendable resource' of the planet which will allow capitalism to continue its headlong course by overstepping the limits mentioned by Sukhdev?

The economist Joseph Schumpeter called crises 'creative destructions'. The current crisis is profound, systemic, global, and takes various forms – at once economic, social and energy and food-related. For the first time, the entire system is encountering its physical limits. What is the solution? The conclusion arising from the analysis is so alarming that one hesitates to name it.

Everything points in the direction of a wave of 'creative destructions' on an unprecedented scale, a wave involving not only the elimination of many material forces of production and irreplaceable natural resources, but also the serious risk of physical destruction of millions of human beings. For this there is a precedent. At the end of the 19th century the combined effects of a series of exceptional droughts and fluctuation of agricultural prices on the world market led to the deaths of millions in India, China, Brazil, Morocco and the Horn of Africa.

American Marxist writer, urban theorist and historian Mike Davis coined the phrase 'tropical genocides' to describe these terrible events.[283] There is a risk that a succession of similar events will take place in the future, but on a much wider scale, and with a difference. This time, rather than floods and droughts being the result of natural phenomena such as El Niño, they will be the direct consequence of the greed of capitalist conglomerates clinging to their excess profits derived from fossil fuels.

The struggle for an alternative is more important and urgent than ever. Militants inevitably think of Rosa Luxemburg's *Socialism or Barbarism*. However, apart from being discredited by Stalinism, the socialist alternative needs to be redefined. The climate question in effect marks the beginning of a new era, both for capitalism and its opponents. No project for emancipation that does not take into account the constraints of its natural limits can be valid.

Chapter Eleven
ECOSOCIALISM – THE ONLY OPTION

Capitalism has taken us down a dead-end and the situation is now critical. Nevertheless, ignoring the profit motive for a moment, we can present the outlines of a rational solution, combining four elements:

1. Satisfying real social needs;
2. Reducing global production by reducing the length of the working week and eliminating the production of useless and harmful goods. Reducing the amount of transport used by a substantial amount (which implies relocation of production);
3. A radical increase of energy efficiency and complete transition to the use of renewables, regardless of cost;
4. The creation of political and cultural conditions for the collective responsibility for production and consumption, through a democratic process.

These four elements are inter-dependent. Meeting basic human needs will determine how global production is reduced. This in its turn influences the transition to renewables. Reducing working hours is a prerequisite for the effective exercise of democracy by producers and this completes the circle by creating the conditions necessary for a collective redefinition of needs which have been alienated by commercial production.

These four aims must be achieved together, on a global scale, and in a very short period of time. This will not be easy but it can be achieved. The major difficulty is political because these four goals are inconceivable without a series of deep incursions into capitalist property. These goals require the expropriation of the monopolies in the energy sector and the confiscation of their assets; democratic planning of the transition at all levels; radical extension of the public sector, in particular in the domains of transport and housing and making basic services free. A global fund for adaptation would be created, under the control of social movements in developing countries. There would need to be public funding of research and a halt to its appropriation by industry; expropriation of the banks and credit agencies so that the necessary funds for transition could be in the hands of the collective; and a cut in profits so that the reduction in working hours could take place without loss of pay, with a reduction of shift work and compensatory hiring. Also necessary would be a democratic agrarian reform with decentralisation of most food production by the supporting of peasant agriculture. It may be argued that this is easier said than done. True, but without this strong medicine, it will be impossible to avoid both climate disaster and the increase in dangerous technologies. The first thing to do is to spell this out clearly!

In the abstract and considered in isolation, these necessary measures are not completely incompatible with the functioning of the capitalist system. For example, at given moments in their history, several influential countries have put their energy industry into public ownership. But uniting these measures into a coherent plan achievable within two generations is inconceivable within the framework of 'pure capitalism' as described by Marxist economist Michel Husson.[284] The programme of transition towards a truly sustainable society cannot be implemented without putting on the agenda, in all principal domains, the replacement of production for profit by production for social use to meet basic human needs which are democratically decided.

There is no point in beating about the bush: this transition corresponds to a socialist transformation. However, the ecological record of the USSR, Eastern Europe and China, which called themselves 'socialist', or still do, is disastrous. Furthermore, supporters of socialism of all variants continually show that they have difficulty in grasping the ecological challenge and responding appropriately. We must therefore ask whether there is an insurmountable defect inherent in socialist theory in general and in Marxism in particular.

This problem is not new. Already in 1979, the philosopher Hans Jonas was asking in *The Imperative of Responsibility*, whether Marxism or capitalism is better for warding off ecological danger.[285] He begins by leaning towards Marxism, because, he argues, it is based on 'collective needs' rather than on profit which 'creates needs'. Also, as 'a tyranny of asceticism', Marxism is the best option to 'impose the unpopular choices which the threats of the future demand'. But in further discussion of whether these potential advantages could be transformed into a genuinely better method, the author goes on to list the basic reasons why, all things considered, socialism would in reality be far worse for the environment than any other system.

The most important of these reasons is the status of technology. For Jonas, technology in itself imposes a heavy intrinsic burden, independent of social systems and is the fundamental cause of environmental destruction. As the aim of socialism is 'to further liberate technology from the hindrances of capitalism', he takes the opposite view and declares more or less that 'the capitalist hindrances to technological progress should be maintained'.[286] And especially, Jonas concludes, it would be a mistake to end private ownership of the means of production. It is true that this is the cause of the alienation of the workers from the products of their labour, but the abolition of this alienation and expropriating the expropriators would allow technology that has been liberated to become even more invasive because it has been collectivised in the service of 'human bliss'.

Jonas pursues his argument to its ultimate political conclusion. He insists that Ernst Bloch's *The Principle of Hope* – the aspiration towards a better world – constitutes the most formidable threat to the environment because this Utopia implies the unachievable promise of a better life for the greatest number. Anticipating many authors in vogue today in certain sectors of the zero-growth movement, Jonas concludes that 'restriction rather than growth will have to be the keyword, and this will be much more difficult for preachers of Utopia than for pragmatists who are not bound by ideology'.

This book by Jonas, a veritable best-seller, has had an enormous influence, direct or indirect, throughout the green movement. On re-reading it one is struck by the fact that the terms of the debate between the Left and what one might call, for want of a better term, political and associative ecology, have hardly developed at all. In spite of its diversity, the ecological movement shares three of Jonas's key ideas, namely that:

1. Respect for ecological balance requires in the first instance reduction of consumption. The sphere of production is not considered, as if over-consumption did not result from over-production.
2. Protection of the environment, therefore, depends above all on an ethic of individual frugality and moderation. As it is hardly likely that the majority will accept the necessary restrictions, decision-makers must be ready to impose them, by subterfuge or by force.
3. Socialism is a sort of super-productivism, more ecologically destructive than capitalism, because it promises material abundance to the greatest number, while the ecological crisis makes austerity the order of the day.

Jonas can certainly take the credit for having asked the question about responsibility towards future generations. But he does it with reference to the patriarchal idea that protection of the child by the father constitutes the basis of all ethics, and that this model should be the guide for government actions. The moralising and potentially authoritarian nature of his thought is evident. Its religious dimension becomes obvious when he states that 'Nature cultivates values because it cultivates aims'.[287]

This religious dimension is directly linked to the focus on consumption, and stresses resistance to temptation as the individual spur to a change in behaviour. For Jonas, socialism is what used to exist in Eastern Europe behind the Iron Curtain. While he credits it with producing for 'collective needs', he is in effect pointing to uniform greyness and austerity imposed by 'tyranny'. At the same time he is too ready to attribute diversity of tastes and needs to the 'creation of needs' by the market. According to Jonas, a return to religion would help to extricate us from the ecological crisis, by returning monkish asceticism and respect for divine creation to their former glory.

It is hardly surprising to find similar ideas about the climate in a document produced by European bishops which is mentioned at the beginning of Jonas' book. But let us make no mistake, these ideas are found in many other places as well, albeit in a perhaps less extreme form. Indeed, since it is focussed on consumption, almost all the mass-produced ideology on the environmental question more or less subscribes to the ideology of restriction and repentance represented by *The Responsibility Principle*. Yann Arthus Bertrand's film *Home*, for instance, is basically no more than an exhortation to everyone, rich or poor, bourgeois or proletariat, to become involved in ecology so as to obtain forgiveness for their sins and for those of the human race.[288]

Jared Diamond's best-seller *Collapse* shares some of the same basic assumptions; that unless we consume less and have fewer children we will incur terrible punishments. As if to emphasise the inadequacy of structural responses, Diamond contrasts the excellent ecological balance sheet of a private oil company (Chevron) to the awful waste by a public enterprise (the Indonesian national oil company PERTAMINA). The message is clear: everything is a matter of personal ethics. There is no need to have recourse to collective solutions such as nationalisation of energy resources, extension of the public sector or making basic services free, as these would only exacerbate the situation.

The most extreme ideologies of the religion of ecology lapse easily into eschatology. This is the case with Diamond when he follows the work of American ecologist Peter Vitousek in suggesting that, between now and 2050, human activities will use almost the whole photosynthetic capacity of the biosphere, so that 'only a small amount of solar radiation will be available to enable the growth of natural vegetation'.[289]

In the same context Jonas and many others also have no hesitation in naming Thomas Malthus as the father of ecology.[290] Similarly Garret Hardin, author of an article entitled *The Tragedy of the Commons*, proposes the idea that collective ownership of natural resources is fatal. It leads inevitably to the resources' destruction, he argues, because everyone uses them for their own immediate ends, without considering themselves responsible for the environment or the future.[291] Incapable even of imagining that current individualism could be a product of the capitalist jungle, Hardin raises the selfishness and greed of the petit bourgeoisie to the rank of a characteristic of *Homo sapiens*.

It is relatively easy to unpick all this reactionary ideological clutter embedded in pseudo-science. For instance, we could respond to Hardin by saying that private capitalist property is in the process of destroying irreplaceable resources on a scale unprecedented in the history of the human race, especially by exhausting the supply of fossil fuels which nature has taken several million years to make. But this is not sufficiently convincing, since the record of the Soviet Union and the countries of Eastern Europe shows that a society based on collective ownership of the means of production can be just as damaging to the environment, or even more so, than one based on private property. In this respect, the records on the climate question cannot be denied. Just before the fall of the Berlin Wall, Czechoslovakia was emitting 20.7 tonnes of CO_2 per person per annum, whilst the German Democratic Republic was emitting 22 tonnes. In comparison, the USA, Canada and Australia – the most significant emitters of CO_2 in the developed capitalist world – were emitting respectively 18.9, 16.2 and 15 tonnes of CO_2 per person per annum, with a much greater GNP.[292]

In order not to draw erroneous conclusions from these figures, we must return to the definition of socialism as a society which production is democratically planned to meet human needs. In this context, the USSR and its satellites (not to mention contemporary China, experiencing a capitalist boom under the auspices of the bureaucracy) were neither socialist nor communist, but states blocked on the road of transition to a post-capitalist mode of production. Logically therefore, we must ask ourselves whether the environmental damage in these countries was the result of their new socialist characteristics, or from the legacies of capitalism, or from hybrid forms of the two systems.

We have identified the accumulation of capitalism under the impetus of competition for profit as the basic cause of damage to the environment, and we have used the rather vague term of 'productivism'. Productivism may be defined as 'production for the sake of production' and 'consumption for the sake of consumption'. The two are evidently complementary, and it is worth noting that Marx considers them as characteristic of the degeneration of capitalism.

In *Theories of Surplus Value* Marx argues '...while the over-production of the worker is production for others,[293] capitalist production is production for the sake of production.[294] However, as his riches increase, he certainly doesn't reach this ideal and becomes a spendthrift in his turn, even if only to make a display of his riches ... if he enjoys his riches, it is always with a bad conscience; he does it for the ulterior motive of savings and accounts. The capitalist becomes more or less incapable of fulfilling his mission once he desires the accumulation of pleasure rather than the pleasure of accumulation. So he too is a producer of over-production. This over-production must have its accompanying over-consumption; consumption for the sake of consumption must complement production for the sake of production'.[295]

The USSR was not capitalist, but was it productivist? In a certain sense, yes. The economy was bureaucratically planned by political leaders, who adopted under Stalin the absurd dogma of 'socialism in one country' and then, under Khrushchev, adopted the insane aim of 'catching up with and overtaking the USA'. The state enterprises were run by directors appointed from above. Encouraged to comply with of the targets of the plan with individual bonuses, proportional to the amount of materials used, these *managers* had a personal interest in burning the maximum amount of carbon and in building machines – for instance tractors for agriculture – using the maximum amount of steel produced.

This system of bonuses is clearly inspired by capitalism, not socialism. Furthermore, it is effectively productivist, encouraging production for the sake of production. Nevertheless, this productivism is different from the productivism that inspires the market economy. Capitalists would seek to burn less coal and consume less steel for each item produced in order to reduce their costs and increase their share of the market. In other words they would want over-consumption to absorb the over-production. These considerations were of no interest to managers under the Soviet system who were not concerned with the final product. We are thus dealing with a hybrid form which could be termed bureaucratic productivism. It is a less effective copy of the capitalist original and thus less socially legitimate (remember the queues outside the state-run shops!) but it is just as destructive.

Does the sad story of the pollution caused in the German Democratic Republic and Czechoslovakia mean that Jonas was partly correct, that, all things considered, capitalism is the least worst for the environment of all the 'currently existing' systems? No, because the constant pursuit of surplus profit drives capitalism to unremittingly increase labour productivity, to produce ever more items. Thus, although starting from different bases, in the final analysis the two systems both imply increased over-consumption of materials, leading to increased emissions of greenhouse gases. But the similarities end there. In fact, a collective economy cannot function sustainably without democracy among the producers and the extension of this democracy to the entire planet. The collapse of the Soviet Union and its satellites was thus inevitable. The despotic political system on the one hand, and the strategy of 'peaceful co-existence' with global capitalism on the other, were in opposition to the material base of the society.

However, an economy driven by profit destroys the environment according to an implacable logic. This would be in perfect balance with its own laws so it would be foolish to expect it to collapse of its own accord. On an historical scale, capitalism is without doubt the most 'ecocidal' of modes of production.

Tsarist Russia was a backward country and the Soviet Union was battered and surrounded by threatening enemies after the First World War, and then the Civil War. From the point of view of technology, its economy would not have got off the ground without coal. Certainly after 1945, the level of science and technology would have allowed for the exploration of other energy sources but the regime chose not to do this. One of the reasons was the existence of the privileged bureaucracy and its *sui generis* productivism. Under a one-party regime, based on a chain of command, it would have been dangerous to call upon the creativity of researchers, or of the population in general, or to call for the decentralisation of production.

The development of renewables implies creativity, participation and decentralisation, yet there was no question of this for the *nomenklatura* which was determined to copy capitalist technology. One of the most catastrophic results of this was Chernobyl, a monstrous hybrid of capitalist technology and bureaucratic productivism.

To conclude, the responsibility of the USSR and its satellites for environmental damage cannot be denied, but this does not invalidate the description of the climate tipping-point as capitalist. The responsibility cannot be laid at the door of socialism, a system which has not yet been achieved anywhere. It is due to the formation of a parasitic social sector – a bureaucracy – which, in order to protect its material privileges and its monopoly of power, created a despotic regime, renounced global socialism and aped both capitalist technologies and capitalist organisational systems.

One of the flaws in Jonas's reasoning, which demonstrates the profoundly reactionary side of his thinking, is that he saw the dictatorship of the Soviet apparatchiks as a possible reference point for ecological politics, whereas it was precisely this dictatorship which created the problem. In the face of the environmental challenge the two advantages of Marxism (according to *The Principle of Responsibility*) are not those identified by Jonas, but production for real needs (which cannot be reduced to 'collective needs'), and democracy among producers. Without the second, the first cannot function – real needs cannot even be identified.

For Jonas, the USSR was nothing less than the application of Marxist theories. One might ask whether Jonas had read the author of *Capital* or if he only knew his Stalinist epigones. For instance, the Marxist formulation on the subject of capitalist limits to development does not refer to 'liberation of technology', as Jonas claims, but to the liberation of productive forces, including immaterial forces. Education, co-operation, knowledge, public health, all are productive forces, and their liberation causes no environmental damage. Furthermore, one will search Marx's writings in vain to discover anything implying that the despotism of the *nomenklatura* corresponded to his desire to find everywhere a government similar to the Paris Commune, an elected body which included the representatives of several political parties...

Over the course of time and as a result of various events, distinctions developed within the socialist workers' movement. Communists split from social democrats, and then split into various tendencies; pro- and anti-Stalinists, for instance. This distinction survives today in the form of differences between productivists and anti-productivists, or ecosocialists. Apart from their disagreements, these families and sub-families still preserve a certain number of common references, a common jargon, etc. A similar process is taking place within the ecology movement. The decision of green parties to manage capitalism has given rise to splits, and we have seen the birth of new, more radical political tendencies, but still characterised by the theoretical framework from which they sprang. The 'de-growth' or 'zero-growth' movement is a product of this division and, as noted above in Chapter 5, we do not share its concepts. The moment has come to open the debate.

In the same vein as Jonas, advocates of de-growth put the principal emphasis on cultural criticism of consumerism. This criticism is necessary, but not sufficient. We believe that the central thrust of the alternative resides in challenging the entire mode of production. In effect, the current mode of production not only generates 'consumption for the sake of consumption' at one extreme but also, and simultaneously, chronic under-consumption at the other. It is thus an illusion to hope that ecological destruction could be avoided by a 'cultural ripple effect' against over-consumption. On the one hand, this movement is more or less confined to developed countries, (where it does not take into account the unsatisfied needs of millions of victims of unemployment, exclusion and casualisation). On the other hand, in the absence of structural changes, individual actions can only result in an ascetic life-style, which is indeed not very 'contagious'.

The only way to prevent a climate tipping point without having recourse to Sorcerer's Apprentice type technologies is a radical reduction of energy consumption, and thus of processing as well as transportation of materials. The advocates of 'de-growth' can be credited with introducing this question into the discussion. Nevertheless, de-growth does not constitute a social project, it is only a quantitative constraint of the transition. It is certainly a major constraint, which issues new challenges to every strategy of social transformation. But the way to meet these challenges is not decided on the qualitative level, and this is precisely what explains the co-existence of diametrically opposed left and right 'de-growth' currents.

Whether we wish to or not, we must make a decision for or against capitalism. Some opponents of growth avoid the question. In 2008 the *New Scientist* published an article written in collaboration with the economist Herman Daly, one of the leading exponents of de-growth in the English-speaking world.[296] It was a piece of fiction, describing life in the USA ten years after a decision to adopt a form of 'stationary capitalism' which 'does not consume resources faster than they are can be renewed, and does not discard waste faster than it can be absorbed'. Let us leave aside the fact that 'stationary capitalism' is a contradiction in terms, and let us observe that the prospect is rather off-putting. In this society, 'scientists establish the rules' every year, not only for the acceptable quantity of waste, but also for the quota of immigration compatible with the stabilisation of population, the number of children permitted, etc.

Here, just as for Jonas, the radicalisation of a strategy focussed on consumption, based on a patriarchal concept of responsibility, clearly leads to a reactionary outcome; a despotic green capitalism, accompanied by excessive bureaucracy, and where there are still social inequalities. A 'sustainable' society ....where there are still exploiters and exploited, frontiers, expulsions, police and army in the service of the wealthy, etc.

At the same time, anti-capitalist professions of faith are not sufficient to differentiate between the right and left views of de-growth. Serge Latouche, one of the most high-profile spokespeople of this current, boasts an extreme anti-capitalist position, but this covers some very reactionary concepts.[297] This paradox is explained by a fairly unsubtle sleight-of-hand. Latouche amalgamates growth and development, then development and capitalism, so that, when all is said and done, his anti-capitalism is nothing more than a condemnation of human development. In *Survivre au Development,* he starts by stating that development cannot be divorced from its historical context, without which the concept would mean 'everything and its opposite'.[298] Quite! But then, instead of analysing the specific nature of capitalist development, he defines development in general as 'an undertaking designed to transform the relations of people to one another and to nature into commodities'. Now, if we are not to say that this definition applies specifically to capitalist development, then the inventors of stone-cutting, of agriculture and the wheel, who did not produce goods but commodities, are placed in the same category as James Watt and his steam engine, or Bill Gates and his software programmes, and we should be sorry not to have remained at the hunter-gatherer stage...

In support of his argument, Latouche claims that (capitalist) development is the only 'really existing' development, that no other form is possible and that 'another type of development would be nonsense'. This is sophistry. It could equally well be argued that the only really existing form of democracy in the world today is capitalist, that no other form is possible. Similarly for justice, liberty, peace, and culture, should we insist on abandoning democracy, justice, liberty, culture? It is evidently absurd. In effect, Latouche's method is identical to that of those on the ultra-left whose universal response is 'Only solution, revolution', and his conclusion is similar: 'Only solution, abandon development'. It appears radical, but in fact is nothing of the sort, because condemning 'development' in general, and amalgamating it with capitalism, in reality enables capitalism to be sidestepped. This system thus loses all historical validity, to the extent that its laws are part of the nature of development. Capitalism is not denounced: 'development' is denounced (improperly assimilated into 'growth').

This condemnation constitutes a dangerous philosophical path, since the capacity for social development is part of human nature. Misanthropy is not far away. It is also a dead-end, since the transformation necessary to escape the climate trap, well and truly requires, for instance, some form of development. Something that has the potential to exist in the current conditions should be allowed to materialise and replace the current circumstances.

In social and political terms, the entire difficulty consists in making this potential future desirable in the eyes of the exploited and the oppressed, who are chained to the machinery of capitalism by the daily obligation to sell their labour-power in exchange for payment, and who naturally hope that growth will guarantee their livelihood. Instead of tackling this problem in concrete terms, Latouche avoids it and gambles on the 'pedagogy of catastrophes', which, 'however unpleasant it may be', will 'allow for the necessary change of vision, a condition for the triumph of the alternatives'. This 'pedagogy' does rather smack of Malthus, and Latouche, like Jonas, makes no attempt to conceal this when he argues 'the carrying capacity of the earth has been greatly exceeded'.[299] He doesn't tell us how many human lives should disappear for the pedagogy to be effective.

The 'anti-growth' current rejects this 'pedagogy of catastrophes', and is searching for a social strategy to attract the popular layers of society in the fight against capitalist productivism. Its main angle of attack continues to be moderation of consumption. Paul Aries, for example, discusses 'ways of making rationing desirable'. But one of the proposals is that water for satisfying basic needs should be free.[300] This is a demand which the Left should support unreservedly, and which leaves the individual sphere to introduce the problem at the social level. Similar demands should be made in the field of energy and other vital resources; making these free would have an enormous anti-productivist and anti-consumerist impact. Nevertheless, it is obvious that such demands conflict with the logic of profit, and therefore with the private possession of resources and of means of production. For instance, making electricity free for the satisfaction of current needs pre-supposes the public ownership of the energy sector. This also applies in the case of water, and it is clear that such measures imply a redistribution of wealth in favour of the public sector.

Since over-consumption results in the final analysis from over-production, it is the mode of production that needs to be tackled. This requires collective social and political action. Participation of the producers in this is absolutely decisive, but at the same time, it is this that presents the greatest difficulty. Hervé Kempf entitled one of his works, *Pour Sauver la Planète, Sortez du Capitalisme*. The fact that this is cast in the form of an exhortation reinforces the idea that this is a case of personal motivation. Indeed, for Kempf, capitalism is not a society for the generalised production of goods, but 'a state of society in which people are supposed to be motivated only by the search for profit and allow the mechanism of the market to regulate all the activities which connect them'.[301] This peculiar definition of a mode of production by motivation and the consent of individuals, instead of by its economic basis, leads logically to a strategy of exit from the system by individuals or small groups.

Kempf argues, 'Leaving capitalism behind means recognising other motivations besides individual self-interest; it also means removing the economy – production and exchange of goods – from its central place in society, and replacing it with the organisation of harmonious human relationships'. It may appear attractive to want to remove the economy from its central place in society. The problem is that the human race produces its existence socially, and that the current mode of production is precisely the cause of environmental destruction. It is therefore a question of fighting it collectively, not of bypassing it.

The key question is that of the interconnection between economic struggles and those for the protection of the environment. In a general sense, advocates of 'de-growth' are not interested in immediate demands for pay and jobs, which they consider consumerist. They are mistaken. In reality, the more defensive and scattered the struggles are, the more the relationship of power is stacked against the workers, and the less are workers able to support anti-capitalist solutions, which are essential for breaking the productivist spiral.

When workers accumulate immediate victories against the management, then, being emboldened and gaining self-awareness, they can make more advanced demands against capitalist property. This, of course, is not in itself enough to develop ecological awareness. But it is only by collectively reclaiming their means of production that the exploited and oppressed can reclaim eventually the basic means of production – nature and its resources – from which they were separated by developing capitalism. And it is only via this process that they can develop responsible management of the environment, without the need for an uncontrollable bureaucracy. In a general sense, only a strategy based on the self-management of social production and of our relationship with nature can allow us to envisage a democratic solution to the problem which worries Jonas and the advocates of 'de-growth' – the fact that 'Late Capitalism' has created on a mass scale, in developed countries, a certain amount of needs and habits which should be critically examined, as they are ecologically unsustainable.

This strategy could build a bridge between today's social resistance movements and a society that is sustainable in the true sense of the word. I have experienced this myself. In the 1970s, I lent my support to a group of several hundred redundant workers in the glass-blowing industry, whose workplace had been closed after a long and radical struggle against the multinational owners. They were finally able to put their collective re-training to use in a public firm providing thermal insulation and house-renovation. The business was undermined from all sides and did not last very long, but those concerned had the time to develop an authentically ecosocialist argument in favour of moderation in energy consumption and, especially, to show solidarity with opponents of nuclear power stations.

History presents us with numerous examples demonstrating that the most lasting environmental empowerment is that which develops from self-management by the working class, thus from a position of strength in the class struggle and the self-awareness that results from this. Older examples are also interesting. This proposal for managing the forest resources monopolised by feudal overlords was written during the German Peasants' Revolt in 1525; 'Our fifth complaint is the problem of wood-cutting, because our masters have appropriated all the woods for their sole use, and if a poor man needs anything, he has to buy it at double the price. We believe that all the woods ... should again become common property, and it should be possible for any member of the community to take what he needs without paying for it ...; he should merely inform a local committee elected for this purpose; exploitation will thus be avoided'.[302] This is a remarkable text. Five centuries ago, humble peasants proposed the establishment of an elected body to prevent over-exploitation of the commons. This puts Hans Jonas's 'ascetic tyranny' and Garret Hardin's 'tragedy of the commons' in their place.

From the ideological standpoint, we should be very sceptical about right-wing advocates of 'de-growth such as Latouche. From a scientific point of view, one can only express disagreement with the 'fourth principle of thermodynamics' propounded by the economist Nicholas Georgescu-Roegen, according to whom the increase of entropy (measure of disorder) is a fundamental characteristic of life, and even of matter.[303] From the standpoint of the perception of social reality, it is a question of freeing oneself from the unilateral view of wage earners as agents of over-consumption, complicit in the destruction of the planet, instead of exploited producers, whose collective action could be an agent of change, bringing into question their own alienated mode of consumption. Having said this, credit is due to Georgescu-Roegen for having been one of the first to denounce the myth of infinite material growth in a finite world, and the advocates of de-growth are right on one key issue. The priority for stabilising the climate is not the introduction of new green technologies, but the reduction of energy consumption, thus of the production and transport of goods. This is something that Marxists are reluctant to accept. This brings us therefore to the second question posed at the beginning of this chapter. Apart from Stalinist caricatures, is there some unacceptable flaw in socialist theory in general, and Marxism in particular?

Even when they have not read him – which is often the case – Greens never fail to repeat that Marx is productivist and rejects any idea of a limit to resources. This view does not stand up to critical examination. It is true that some of the formulations by Marx and Engels are ambiguous and debatable – but the question of natural resources and their limits is very well represented in their analysis. Marx explicitly says that it is the finite amounts of soil, minerals, water-power and other resources which have made it possible for property owners to monopolise them, with all that results from this; the separation of producers from the land, the formation of a class forced to sell their labour-power to the owners of the means of production, and the chance for the landowners of the earth to divert a part of the global surplus-value in the form of unearned income. In other words, without natural limits capitalism is not possible.[304]

More fundamentally, a serious appraisal of Marxist thought cannot ignore the concept of 'rational regulation of the exchange of matter' (or 'social metabolism') between humanity and nature, as discussed in *Capital*. The point of departure for this elaboration is very prosaic. Thanks to the work of Liebig (the pioneer of soil chemistry), Marx had grasped that capitalist urbanisation breaks the nutrient cycle; human and animal waste are not returned to the earth, the soil is deprived of minerals, and the resulting loss of fertility cannot be restored on an historic scale. Marx loved scientific discussions, and he was passionate about this question of agronomics. In fact he goes further and poses the general question of 'exchange of matter' between human beings and the environment. And he does it within the framework of the relationship between 'the realm of freedom' and that of 'necessity', in other words on the limits to freedom possible in relation to labour.

There is nothing more incorrect than seeing Marxism as the promise of a society of idlers carousing to their hearts' content, thanks to the replacement of workers by robots. Such an idea is completely foreign to Marx's thought. Work for him is a categorical imperative – the particular relationship between humanity and the environment – and the finite nature of resources implies that increases in the productivity of human labour as a resource is not infinite.[305] He deduces from this that the 'only possible freedom' resides in the 'rational management' of the exchange of matter between our species and its environment. With this concept in mind, he returns to the question of the soil, reaching the conclusion that the separation between town and country – indeed, between production and consumption of agricultural products on a global scale – must be abolished.[306] This methodology bears comparison with the best contemporary concepts of global environmental problems.[307] Among ecologists, Barry Commoner is, as far as I know, the only one who has done Marx justice on this point.[308] Nevertheless, the idea of the rational regulation of the human/nature metabolism seems tailor-made for understanding climate change, as the disruption of the carbon cycle described in Chapter 2 constitutes a textbook case of 'irrational management of the exchange of matter'.

In fact, Marx is much more of an 'ecologist' than many of his successors realise. The exceptions to this are John Bellamy Foster and Paul Burkett; for them, ecology is 'at the heart of Marxism'.[309] These two writers have the credit for rehabilitating 'Marx's ecology', but they tend to go too far in the other direction. Indeed, if ecology were really at the heart of Marxism, we would need to explain why all currents of Marxist thought missed the opportunity to engage with the ecological question during the 1960s and 1970s. I feel that it is pointless to exaggerate: the concept of 'rational regulation of exchange between humanity and nature' is authentically ecological, but a global vision of the ecological dimension of a socialist transformation is only briefly apparent in Marx's thought. Furthermore, in my opinion, this vision is undermined by a serious error in the field of energy resources.

It is striking that in their analysis of the Industrial Revolution, Marx and Engels have simply failed to grasp the enormous ecological and economic potential of the transition from a renewable source of energy, produced by photosynthesis of solar radiation – wood – to a fossil fuel source, produced by the fossilisation of solar radiation and thus exhaustible in a historical time period – coal. Let us make no mistake: in the eyes of Marx, technology is not neutral. He makes a clear distinction between pre-industrial and industrial technologies, 'specifically capitalist' according to his definition.[310] But this distinction is absent from the field of energy sources, as if these could be neutral. It is true that during Marx's lifetime the same steam engine could be powered either by wood or by coal, so that the relative importance of the energy sources was not obvious. But it has become clear in the course of capitalist technological development.

Today it is incontrovertible. If we compare the thermal sectors with the nuclear sector, it is obvious that different sources of energy require different technologies, and that the choice of technology is not neutral. Accepting the neutral nature of energy sources, as in the case of some who claim to be Marxists but support nuclear energy, boils down to putting oneself in opposition to a fundamental premise of historical materialism – the historically and socially determined nature of technology.

By definition, energy is the *sine qua non* of all labour, of all human activity. However negligible it may be, an error at this level cannot but acquire a systemic character. This is why we may say that the energy question represents a veritable Trojan horse in 'Marx's Ecology' and in Marxism in general, in all its various tendencies. For Marx himself, the confusion between energy flow and energy storage did not lead to direct consequences; it is more of a blind spot or a shadow zone. But this conceals the existence of the fact that in Marxism there are two blueprints.

The first blueprint is a cyclical, progressive one. Starting from the issues of the soil, *Capital* proposes the basis of an authentic socio-ecological concept, based on the idea of regulation of the exchange of matter, and the on rational management of natural cycles modified by human impact. This view is not fixed but circular. Humanity transforms nature by taking on, as far as possible, the circulation of exchanges with the environment.

The second blueprint is linear. The cyclical approach applied to the question of the soil is not transferred to the field of energy. Here, since he has not grasped the difference between energy flow and energy supply, Marx accepts *de facto* the utilitarian pattern >resource >use >waste (CO_2) which is that of classic economics. He has no knowledge of the impact because the conditions of the carbon cycle have not been taken into account.

All evidence suggests that these two outlines obey two different logics. The first points towards prudent intervention in the mechanisms of nature ('looking after the earth like a good father looks after his family' as Marx says in *Capital*). The second implies the productivist ambiguity ('growth of productive forces' freed from 'the shackles of capitalist development'). The two are more than contradictory, they are antagonistic. For the system to be coherent, one of the two must give way to the other. The 'ecologisation' of Marxism cannot therefore be achieved simply by the spellbinding rediscovery of 'Marx's ecology' to which John Bellamy Foster invites us. There must be clarification at the very heart of Marxism; we expose the Trojan horse – the confusion between energy flow and energy storage – and its corollary – the linear schema of resource >product > waste.

It goes without saying that the ambiguities of Marx's ecology are far from explaining all the difficulties of Marxism, or of those who claim a Marxist stance on the ecological question. It would be absurd, for instance, to attribute the energy policy of Stalinist regimes to Marx's ambiguities. By the same token, it would be unjust to blame Marx's ambiguous position for the fact that the workers' movement under social-democratic leadership allowed capitalism to mutilate as it chose 'the other source of all wealth' – nature.

It is obvious that Marx's ambiguities on ecology cannot explain all the difficulties that Marxists have with the ecological question. Furthermore, examination of the intellectual production of Marxism in the 20th century reveals that the antagonism between the two approaches has been resolved in practice simply by the disappearance of the first. Very quickly, without discussion, the linear model has been accepted as the exclusive model – rather more easily no doubt as the problem of the soil seemed to have been resolved by the invention of chemical fertilisers. Although Lenin referred to it in some of his discussions on the agrarian question,[311] and Bukharin made an intelligent presentation of it in his handbook on Historical Materialism,[312] the Marxist concept of the rational regulation of material exchanges subsequently sank into oblivion. No Marxist thinker assigned to it the importance it deserves, and in fact none of them saw its relevance when the ecological question became a social issue in the 1960s. This is not the place to enquire into the reasons for this discontinuity in revolutionary Marxism. It is sufficient to warn the reader against simplistic interpretations: Stalinism is not the sole culprit, although in this field, as well as others, it introduced a terrible theoretical regression. Anti-Stalinist Marxists such as Trotsky also forgot Marx's bold revolutionary anticipation of the necessity of rational management of the exchange of matter. Ernest Mandel, a seasoned Marxist, is a striking example. He was aware of the Marxist concept of 'social metabolism' but obviously did not know how to use it in the debate on 'zero growth' launched by the Mansholt Report.[313]

The 'ecologisation' of Marxism requires much more than a simple 'integration' of ecological questions with the anti-capitalist struggle. It is not enough to understand better the ecological stakes, to develop ecological demands and to participate in actions in defence of the environment. All this is desirable, of course, but it is not the heart of the matter. This framework is too narrow. The necessity of escaping from it is clearly demonstrated in the light of climate change. Global warming, in fact is not a strictly environmental problem but a global challenge. Of all environmental phenomena, it is this which most clearly demonstrates that humanity today produces not only its social existence but at the same time the nature which surrounds and conditions that existence – on a planetary scale. Consequently, an anti-capitalist programme worthy of the name must allow the exploited and oppressed to determine not only the society but also the environment they want for themselves and their children.

In view of the relationship between these two aspects, the real challenge is not to integrate ecology into socialism, but rather to integrate socialism into ecology. If this formulation is deliberately provocative, it is because the problem we are confronting is a radically new one; whilst all socialist ventures in the 20th century took place in contexts of under-development of the forces of material production, today the transition towards a non-capitalist mode of production must of necessity involve a reduction of those forces, at least in the developed capitalist countries.

The Transitional Programme written by Leon Trotsky in 1938 begins with the statement that 'The economic prerequisite for the proletarian revolution has already in general achieved the highest point of fruition that can be reached under capitalism'. It concludes that 'The objective prerequisites... have not only 'ripened'; they have begun to get somewhat rotten. Without a socialist revolution, in the next historical period at that, a catastrophe threatens the whole culture of mankind.' The founder of the Red Army refers firstly, of course, to the historical context: the victory of fascism and Nazism, the crushing of the Spanish revolution, and the imminent world war. His judgment on the putrefaction of the objective conditions, however, seems to have broader historical implications. This theme reappears, moreover, in Ernest Mandel's writing: 'Growing productive forces with growing commodity-money relationships can in fact move a society farther from the socialist goal instead of bringing it closer.'[314]

A remarkable quotation, the strategic implications of which deserve to be explored. For this is, in fact, the unprecedented situation with which we are confronted: in the developed countries, capitalism has gone too far in the way it develops material productive forces, such that a worthy socialist alternative implies no longer an advance, but a form of retreat. We are referring to the material forces, and not questioning the need for developing knowledge and cooperation among producers, of course. This retreat of the productive forces in the North – which is possible only with a radical redistribution of wealth – is also essential for a development of the South. It is this new historical conjuncture that is expressed in the pressing need to produce and transport less, and to transfer clean technologies, in order to consume much less energy and totally eliminate fossil CO_2 emissions by the end of this century.

The fact that the development of the material productive forces has begun to move us objectively further from a socialist alternative is the major fact on which the new concept of ecosocialism is founded and justified. Far from being only a new label on the bottle, this concept introduces at least five that need to be considered.

Firstly, the concept of 'humanity's conquest of nature' must be abandoned. The complexity, the unknown forces and the evolutionary character of the biosphere imply a degree of irreducible uncertainty. The interweaving the social and environmental fields must be thought of as a process in constant flux, like a production of nature.

Secondly, the classic definition of socialism must be updated. The only socialism truly possible from now on is that which satisfies real human needs (freed from the alienation of the market), democratically determined by those affected, taking care to examine carefully the environmental impact of these needs and of the manner in which they are met.

Thirdly, we must go beyond the compartmentalised, utilitarian, linear concept of nature as the physical platform from which humanity operates, like the shop where it gets the resources necessary for the production of its social existence and the dump where it deposits the waste products of this activity. Nature is all of these things at once – platform, shop, recycling centre and the totality of living processes which, thanks to the input of solar energy, cause matter to circulate and continually reorder it. Waste products and their disposal must be compatible, both in quality and quantity, with the recycling capacity of ecosystems, so as not to upset the working of the biosphere. This depends on the number and the diversity of biological agents, and also on the quality and complexity of the multiple chain reactions which link them together. In the final analysis, it is the equilibrium of flux which determines the supply of resources for humanity.

Fourthly, energy sources and methods of energy conversion used to satisfy human needs are not socially neutral. Consequently, socialism cannot use Lenin's definition of 'Soviets plus electricity'. The history of climate change and its causes corroborates this; a mode of production is characterised not only by the relationship between production and property, but also by technological sectors, created by choice of energy. The capitalist energy system is centralised, anarchical, wasteful, inefficient, intensively mechanised, based on non-renewable resources and geared towards the underlying over-production of goods. A socialist transformation worthy of the name would necessitate its destruction and its replacement by a decentralised system, planned, economical, efficient, labour intensive, based exclusively on renewable sources and geared towards sustainable production for use and recycling. This does not refer only to energy 'production' in the narrow sense, but to the industrial system as a whole; agriculture, transport, leisure and local planning. The profound historic upheaval could take place in one country or in a group of countries, but can only be finally achieved at a global level, as it presupposes energy self-sufficiency, and especially food self-sufficiency, in different countries and groups of countries. Far from being synonymous with a halt to human development, it implies significant progress in science and technology, as well as the capacity to use them democratically.

Fifthly, in the light of what has been said above, a critical glance should be cast at the increase in the productivity of labour. This incredible increase is the result of the 'destructive progress' of science and technology applied to the perfecting of an unsustainable energy system.[315] In a certain number of domains, the introduction of an ecologically sound anti-capitalist alternative would mean, at least at the beginning, a reduction in mechanisation and the replacement of 'dead' labour by 'living' labour. This is the case in agriculture, where the ultra-mechanised agri-business system, consuming a vast quantity of fertilizers, pesticides and fossil fuel, would need to give way to a different, more labour-intensive method of cultivation. Something similar would apply to the energy sector, because decentralised production based on renewables would involve a lot of work, especially in the area of maintenance. The amount of labour would generally tend to increase radically in a whole series of sectors linked to the environment. A parallel can be drawn between personal care, education, and other areas in which the Left takes it as read that they will be in the public sector; in fact, human intelligence and emotions, combined with a 'caring' culture, are needed in all fields which hinge directly upon the management of, and interaction with, the biosphere.

Some 15 years after Francis Fukuyama unilaterally decreed 'the end of history', an anti-capitalist outcome is needed more than ever. It can only be of a socialist and anti-productivist nature, as we need a simultaneous response to the social and the ecological crisis. The concept of ecosocialism is a response to this unprecedented double emergency.[316] It is based on the logic of Marx's discussion of the 'social metabolism' but broadens it and draws new conclusions in terms of demands, tasks and programme. It takes up the ethical torch carried by William Morris, a friend of Engels, who denounced 'the ghastly stupidity' of a system 'which now bids us all for the sake of life to destroy the reasons for living'.[317] Ecosocialism is anything but a concession to fashion; it is a challenge for the convergence of the struggles. The only possible freedom is rational management, on a co-operative basis, of the exchange of matter between humanity and nature ...with prudent consideration of nature's complexities. The only possible socialism is ecosocialism which is a focussed expression of the fight against the exploitation of human labour and the destruction of natural resources by capitalism – from now on these two strands are indivisible. Ecosocialism does not stem from a romantic vision of establishing 'harmony' between humanity and nature, but from the conviction that true wealth resides in creative activity, in free time, in social relations, and in the contemplation of the world with wonder.

NOTES

1. These ideas were developed in *Les fondements d'une strategie écosocialiste* (Foundations of an ecosocialist strategy), Daniel Tanuro, 2011, http://www.europe-solidaire.org/spip.php?article20954.
2. Karl Marx, *Theories of Surplus Value*.
3. Karl Marx, *The Grundisse*.
4. Ester Boserup, *The conditions of agricultural growth: the economics of agrarian change under population pressure*, Allen & Unwin, London, 1965.
5. Michaël Löwy and Jean-Marie Harribey, *Capital contre nature* (Marx versus nature), PUF, Paris, 2003.
6. 'Large-scale industry and large-scale mechanised agriculture work together. If originally distinguished by the fact that the former lays waste and destroys principally labour-power, hence the natural force of human beings, whereas the latter more directly exhausts the natural vitality of the soil, they join hands in the further course of development in that the industrial system in the countryside also enervates the labourers, and industry and commerce on their part supply agriculture with the means for exhausting the soil.', Karl Marx, *Capital*, Vol. 3, Ch. 47.
7. Joel Kovel, *The Enemy of Nature: The end of capitalism or the end of the world?* Zed Books, London, 2002.
8. On the Mayas and China, read the contributions in *Questioning collapse. human resilience, ecological vulnerability and the aftermath of the empire*, Ed. by Patricia McAnany & Norman Yoffee, Cambridge University Press, 2010. On the Incas and Egypt, read *Histoire des agricultures du monde, du Néolithique à la crise contemporaine* (History of world agriculture, from the Neolithic to the contemporary crisis), Seuil, Paris, 1997.
9. Jean-Marie Harribey, *L'Économie économe: le développement soutenable par la réduction du temps de travail* (A thrifty economy sustainable by working less), L'Harmattan, Paris, 1997
10. United Nations Environment Programme, UN conference on Sustainable Development, Rio de Janeiro, 2012.
11. 'Ecologie, luttes sociales et projet révolutionnaire pour le 21e siècle' (Ecology, social struggles and revolutionary project for the 21st century), in *Pistes pour un anticapitalisme vert* (Leads towards a Green anticapitalism), co-ordinator Vincent Gay, Syllepse, Paris, 2010.
12. *Summaries for decision makers*, UNEP, 2007.The IPCC's evaluative reports consist of two types of summaries; technical reports and others aimed at the decision-makers. The latter are adopted after lengthy discussions between the authors of the scientific reports and representatives of governments.

13 Translator's note: in English in the original.
14 Kuhn T.S., *The structure of scientific revolutions*, University of Chicago Press, Chicago, Illinois, 1962.
15 Lawmakers hear of interference in global warming science, *International Herald Tribune*, Paris, 30 January 2007. See also the website of the Union of Concerned Scientists www.ucsusa.org.
16 *International Herald Tribune*, Paris, 1 February 2007.
17 *The Guardian*, London, 2 February 2007.
18 Revelle R. and Suess H., 'Carbon dioxide exchange between atmosphere and ocean and the question of an increase of atmospheric CO_2 during the past decades'. *Tellus 9*, 18-27, Stockholm, 1957.
19 Methane (CH_4) is produced by the decomposition of organic matter in the absence of oxygen (in marshes, animal digestive systems, etc.) Nitrous oxide (N_2O) is a natural product of the activity of certain microbes in the soil, but also, and especially, a gas released by excessive use of nitrogenous fertilizer. Ozone (O_3), which forms on the ground as a result of pollution (tropospheric ozone, not to be confused with the ozone layer of the stratosphere) also contributes to the greenhouse effect, as do a series of industrial gases (perfluorocarbides, hydrofluorocarbons and sulphur hexafluoride). These are present in minute amounts, but their longevity and their contribution to the greenhouse effect are sometimes very important, and their quantities are rapidly increasing.
20 James Lovelock, *The Gaia hypothesis*, 1979, http://www.jameslovelock.org/page34.html.
21 See Peter Westbroek, *Vive la terre - physiologie d'une planète* (Long live earth - physiology of a planet), Scuil, Paris, 1998.
22 Lovelock's Gaia hypothesis is fruitful as a metaphor, but the 'as if' must be insisted upon. Those who interpret the hypothesis literally slip easily into a new form of worship of Nature as a goddess. From here it is only one step to believing that true Nature is without humans. Lovelock himself is not far from taking this view.
23 CH_4: methane.
24 Another argument of climate-change sceptics is that evaporation is responsible for 60% of the natural greenhouse effect. This is true. But the greenhouse effect must not be confused with the *increase* in greenhouse effect. Human activity only has a negligible effect on the amount of water vapour in the air. Furthermore, water vapour does not accumulate: above a certain concentration, droplets condense and fall as rain. CO_2 does not act in the same way. That is why CO_2 is primarily responsible for current global warming.
25 *IPCC Climate Change 2007, Synthesis report*, page 39, fig 2.4, www.ipcc.ch.
26 One gigatonne = one billion tonnes.
27 This 'longevity' may increase with global warming; since CO_2 cannot be eliminated except by 'carbon sinks', its persistence in the atmosphere increases as the sinks become saturated.
28 Gérard Mégie and Jean Jouzel, 'Le changement climatique. histoire scientifique et politique, scénarios futurs' (Climate change. scientific and political history, future scenarios), *La Météorologie,* No. 42, Saint Mande, France, August 2003

29 *Summary for Decision Makers*, UNEP, 2007. NB: The temperature deviations are given with reference to 1999 and should be increased by 0.7°C with reference to the pre-industrial period.
30 Lyme disease is a bacterial infection that is spread to humans by infected ticks. Ticks are tiny, spider-like insects found in woodland areas that feed on the blood of mammals, including humans (Translator's note).
31 IPCC, Climate Change 2007, Contribution of Work Group II, Chapter 9, p. 448.
32 FAO: http://www,fao,org/newsroom/FR/news/2005/102623/index.html
33 Parry et al: 'Millions at risk; defining critical climate threats and targets' in *Global Environmental Change* 11:3, Elsevier, Philadelphia, Pennsylvania, 2001.
34 Contrary to what some climate sceptics assert, uncertainty in estimates is taken very seriously by the IPCC. In drafting its third report in 2001, a special document was entirely devoted to the manner in which the authors had to take this into account.
35 UNDP: *Global Report on Human Development*, 2007-2008, p.94.
36 Parry et al, (2001).
37 UNDP, (2007-2008).
38 UNDP, (2007-2008).
39 These Eight Millennium Objectives for Development, adopted by the UN in 2000, are: to reduce extreme poverty and hunger, ensure primary education for all, equality and autonomy for women, reduction of infant mortality, improvement in maternal health, fight against HIV/AIDS, malaria and other illnesses, ensure a stable environment and establish a global partnership for development.
40 Cecilia Ugaz, 'The fight against climate change; human solidarity in a divided world', quoted in, *Les changements climatiques et la politique Belge de co-operation au développement* (Climate change and the co-operation for development policy of Belgium), Jean-Pascal van Ypersele, SPF Affaires Etrangères, DGCD and UCL, Brussels, 2008.
41 Statement by UNU-EHS (United Nations University Institute for Environment and Human Security) to mark UN Day for Disaster Reduction, 2005.
42 The uncertainty of climate models derives particularly from the very complex role of clouds; on the one hand they contribute to global warming, because they are composed of water-vapour, which is a greenhouse gas; on the other, they reflect the sun's rays into space, it is a question of scientific uncertainty, which could be reduced as knowledge increases. The uncertainty about scenarios of human development is of a different order; it is directly related to socio-political choices.
43 Article in *Science*, quoted in *Le Monde*, Paris, 2 February 2007.
44 Virtue is in the moderate, not the extreme position (Horace).
45 IPCC Climate Change 2007. Contribution of Work Group III, Technical Summary, Table TS.2, page 39.
46 The shelves are enormous plates of ice which extend the glaciers towards the surface of the ocean. Like the glaciers, they are formed by snowfall which is nothing to do with floating ice formed by congealed sea-water. The melting

47 'Antarctic ice shelf collapse tied to global warming', *Environment News Service*, http://www.ens-newswire.com/ens/oct2006/2006-10-16-03.asp , April 2006.
48 'Escalating ice loss found in Antarctica', *Washington Post*, Washington,.14 January 2008.
49 'New concerns on the stability of the west Atlantic ice sheet', *Environment Times*, UNEP, http://www.grida.no/publications/et/pt/page/2559.aspx , 2004.
50 James Hansen et al., *Target atmospheric CO_2: where should humanity aim?*, www.arxiv.org, 2008.
51 Personal communication.
52 *Changements climatiques: grand défi du XXIème siècle*, (Climate change: the great challenge of the 21st century), Conference proceeding, Brussels, 31 March 2009 as part of the Grandes Conferences Catholiques.
53 UN Climate Chief to Visit Antarctica, *ABC News*, 8 January 2008.
54 Bertell Ollman, *La dialectique mise en œuvre* (Dialectics put into practice), Syllepse, Paris, 2005.
55 On the agricultural revolution in the 15th century, read Marcel Mazoyer and Laurence Roudart, *Histoire des agricultures du monde, du Néolithique à la crise contemporaine* (History of world agriculture, from the Neolithic to the contemporary crisis), Seuil, Paris, 1997. On the importance of deforestation and its impact on erosion, read Peter Westbroek, *Vive la terre. Physiologie d'une planète* (Long live earth. physiology of a planet), Seuil , Paris, 1998.
56 See for instance John Bellamy Foster, *The vulnerable planet: a short economic history of the environment.* Monthly Review Press, New York, 1999.
57 'Humans may have prevented super Ice Age', *New Scientist*, London, 12 November 2008.
58 J. Hansen et al, (2008).
59 Apart from it's a historical side, *Collapse* (Penguin, London, 2005) attributes the principal responsibility for the ecological crisis to population growth, thus to the Global South. cf. Daniel Tanuro, 'L'inquiétante pensée du mentor écologiste de Nicolas Sarkozy' (The disturbing ideas of Nicolas Sarkozy's ecology advisor), *Le Monde Diplomatique*, Paris, December 2007. The debate raised by this article can be accessed on-line at http://blog.mondediplo.net/2008-01-18-Effondrement-de-Jared-Diamond
60 Critiques of Diamond's thesis have been advanced, especially by Benny Peiser, 'From ecocide to genocide; the Rape of Rapa Nui', *Energy and Environment*, 16: 3&4, Brentwood, Essex, UK, 2005, and by Terry L. Hunt, 'Rethinking Easter Island's ecological catastrophe', *Journal of Archaeological Science,* Elsevier, Philadelphia, Pennsylvania, 2007, 34: 485-502. See also Daniel Tanuro, 'Catastrophes Écologiques d'hier et d'aujourd'hui: la fausse métaphore de l'Ile de Pâques' (Ecological catastrophes past and present; the false metaphor of Easter Island) in *Critique Communiste* No. 185, Paris, December 2007.
61 In Chapter 11, the responsibility of the former Soviet Union and other non-capitalist economies will be discussed.
62 Nicholas Stern, *Review on the Economics of Climate Change,* 2006, http://

webarchive.nationalarchives.gov.uk/+/http:/www.hm-treasury.gov.uk/sternreview_index.htm.

63 Its combustion releases twice the amount of carbon dioxide than a similar amount of natural gas.
64 Hans Jonas, *The imperative of responsibility*, University of Chicago Press, Illinois, 1985.
65 Rick Sellers, *Renewable energy. Market and policy trends in IEA countries*, International Conference for Renewable Energies, 2004, IEA Side Event.
66 M. C-W. Siemens, 'Utilisation de la chaleur et des autres forces naturelles' (Use of heat and other natural resources), *Revue Scientifique*, No. 10, 5.3.1881. Quoted by F. Iselin, 'Energie solaire, rien de nouveau sous le soleil' (Solar energy, nothing new under the sun) in *SolidaritéS*, No. 48, Geneva, 2004. http://www.solidarites.ch/journal/d/article/1592
67 This is the principle of fuel cells; oxidisation of hydrogen on one electrode and reduction of oxygen on the other allows the production of current when it is needed.
68 Augustin Mouchot, *La chaleur solaire et ses applications industrielles* (Solar heat and its industrial applications), 1869, re-issued 1980, Éditions Blanchard, Paris.
69 Travis Bradford, *Solar revolution. The economic transformation of the global energy industry*, (p.94), MIT Press, Cambridge, Massachusetts, 2006.
70 Nicholas Stern (2006).
71 Paul-André Rosenthal and Jean-Claude Derinck, 'La fabrication du nombre de victimes de la silicose dans les houillières de France de 1946 à nos jours' (The production of the number of victims of silicosis in French coal mines from 1946 to the present day), in *Vingtième Siècle, Revue d'histoire*, No. 95, Presses de Science Po, Paris 2007/3
72 Jean-Marie Chevalier, *Les grandes batailles de l'énergie*, (The big battles for energy), Gallimard, Paris, 2004
73 This figure does not include unearned income from coal and gas.
74 Translator's note: in English in the original.
75 Complete text 23 June 2008, Columbia University: *Global warming twenty years later: tipping points near* http://www.columbia.edu/~jeh1/2008/TwentyYearsLater_20080623.pdf.
76 Matthew Paterson, *Automobile politics*, Cambridge University Press, Cambridge, 2007.
77 Bradford C. Snell, *American ground transport, a proposal for restructuring the automobile, truck, bus & rail industries*, 1974 U.S. Government Report, quoted in Winfried Wolf, *Car mania: a critical history of transport*, Pluto, London, 1996.
78 Daniele Stewart, 'L'Ouest américain menacé par le béton (Concrete threatens the American West), *Le Monde Diplomatique*, Paris, July 2000. Quoted by Paul McGarr, *Why green is red: Marxism and the threat to the environment*, International Socialism Journal, London, Autumn 2000. http://www.marxists.org/history/etol/newspape/isj2/2000/isj2-088/mcgarr.htm.
79 This incredible episode was the subject of a documentary film in 2006 by Chris

Paine, *Who killed the electric car?*

80 Barry Commoner, *The poverty of power: energy and the economic crisis*, Random House, New York, 1976.
81 Oil and coal constitute 38% of maritime goods transport.
82 Office of Science and Technology, Chief Scientific Advisor's Energy Research Group, Report of the Group, 2002.
83 European Commission, http://europa.eu.int/scadplus/leg/fr/lvb/l27021.htm.
84 The report on climate change produced for the Conference of EU Bishops (COMECE) is a good example. The text uses – and misuses – the terms 'moderation', 'humility', 'ascetic' and 'lifestyle'. Particularly significant is this extract from an address by Pope Benedict XVI on global warming. The word 'discipline' appears three times in a single sentence. At the end of his address, His Holiness concludes that discipline 'is a question of responsibility towards Our Lord Who is our Judge; he is our Saviour, but no less our Judge'. *A Christian view of climate change; the implications of climate change for lifestyles and EU politics.* A report to the Bishops of COMECE, October 2008.
85 John Houghton, *Overview of the climate change issue*, 2002, http://www.jri.org.uk/resource/climatechangeoverview.htm.
86 These life spans are approximate and are dependent upon a number of parameters for each different gas. CO_2, the most important greenhouse gas, has no 'lifespan', strictly speaking. It refers to a completely oxidised and stable compound, which cannot be eliminated from the atmosphere except via photosynthesis or by dissolving in the sea. If these 'carbon sinks' are saturated, its lifespan increases.
87 IPCC: Climate Change 2007, Contribution of Working Group III, Technical Summary 2.2., p.39.
88 Part of this rise is already 'in the pipeline', delayed by the thermal inertia of water and ice-masses on the planet.
89 Rajendra Pachauri, *Grandes Conférences Catholiques*, Brussels, 2009.
90 *The Economist*, London, 12 May 2007.
91 To do this, each gas is evaluated in terms of the physical capacity of its molecules to trap infra-red radiation ('irradiative power') on the one hand, and its lifespan in the atmosphere on the other. Since CO_2 is the major greenhouse gas, the quantity of each of the others is expressed in terms of the quantity of CO_2 with the same effect. Methane, for example, has an irradiative power 100 times greater than that of CO_2, but its lifespan is short, so its irradiative power is evaluated as only 25 times greater than CO_2.
92 'Negative emissions' means that ecosystems absorb more CO_2 than they emit.
93 Thus for example Jean-Marie Martin-Amouroux, in his book on the future of the coal industry, mistakenly writes that 'the IPCC's most ambitious scenario' corresponds to 'the target of stabilisation of the maximum concentration of CO_2 in the atmosphere at 450ppm', implying that global emissions should start to reduce by 2020 at the latest, and allows for the temperature increase to be maintained below 2°C. Three assertions, three errors ... Jean-Marie Martin-Amouroux, *Charbon, les métamorphoses d'une industrie. La nouvelle géopolitique du XXIe siècle.* (Coal, metamorphoses of an industry. The new

geopolitics of the 21st century). TECHNIP, Paris, 2008.
94 Figures from 2005, not including emissions from the agriculture and forestry sectors. Source: World Resources Institute.
95 C.L. Weber, G. Peters, D. Guan, K. Hubacek, *The contribution of Chinese exports to climate change*, International Input Output Meeting on Managing the Environment, Seville, 9-11 July 2008.
96 In global terms, it would be advisable to take into account imports by low-wage countries of goods produced in developed countries.
97 *US top greenhouse gas emitter, counting imports*. Reuters, London, 22 July 2009, http://www.reuters.com/article/2009/07/22/idUSLM525876.
98 Swiss Federal Office of the Environment, Climate Section: *Net decline in greenhouse gas emissions in 2007*, 16 April 2009.
99 UN Framework Convention on Climate Change.
100 UNFCCC, article 3.
101 Contribution of Working Group III to IPCC evaluative report, 2007, page 776.
102 This transfer is forecast by UNFCCC, article 4.
103 James Hansen advocates a stabilisation point of below 350 ppm, or even 320 ppm CO_2; significantly less than the 350 ppm of the IPCC, James Hansen et al, (2008).
104 Helmut J. Geist and Eric F. Lambin, W*hat drives tropical deforestation? A meta-analysis of proximate and underlying causes of deforestation based on sub-national case study evidence*, International Geosphere-Biosphere Programme (IGBP) VI. Title VII. Collection; LUCC Report Series 4, Land-Use and Land-Cover Change International Project Office, Louvain-la Neuve, 2001.
105 One example may suffice; while the quantity of recyclable paper and cardboard is estimated at 80%, the effective rate [of recycling] is only 40%, as a global average. Recycling has hardly started to develop in the Global South, and has only reached 44% in the USA. A substantial improvement could be rapidly and simply achieved by co-ordinating modern systems of collection and sorting. A similar result could be obtained for the wood industry, where the obsolescence of products, especially furniture, is evidently planned by the manufacturers.
106 Jos G.J. Olivier et al, *Recent trends in global greenhouse gas emissions; regional trends and spatial distribution of key sources*, Proceedings of the fourth international symposium NSGG-4, Millpress, Rotterdam, 2005.
107 The sun will continue to exist for at least five billion more years.
108 One exajoule = 10^{18} joules
109 UNDP World Energy Council, *World energy assessment; Energy and the challenge of sustainability*, UNDP 2000. The total was obtained by taking into account: identified reserves of oil and those that can be identified in future with 50% probability; proven reserves of gas; estimated reserves of coal. The IPCC report GT III mentions reserves twice the size, but this does not fundamentally modify the conclusions.
110 The differences in temperature on the surface of the earth are the cause of winds and currents, green plants transform solar radiation into chemical energy and water flows towards the sea because solar radiation causes evaporation on the

surface of the oceans, which in turn leads to the formation of clouds, which fall as rain on mountains. Indeed, apart from geothermal energy and tides, all renewable energy is solar.
111 The French chemist Lavoisier (1743-1794) designed a solar kiln using convergent lenses in order to melt metals without causing pollution.
112 http://srren.ipcc-wg3.de/report/srren.
113 UN World Energy Assessment mentions a technical potential 7,600 Exajoules per annum, 18 times greater than global energy needs (op, it, Table 5.26). Researchers from the Stuttgart Thermodynamic Institute suggest an estimate of 5.9: Wolfram Krevitt, Uwe Klann, Stefan Kronshage; *Energy revolution: a sustainable pathway to a clean energy future for Europe*, Institute of Technical Thermodynamics (Stuttgart) and Greenpeace, September 2005.
114 G.P. Harrison and A.R. Wallace, *Climate sensitivity of marine energy*, School of Engineering and Electronics, University of Edinburgh, http://www.era.lib.ed.ac.uk/retrieve/1398/RE+Revised+Final.pdf.
115 L.A. Vega, Ocean Thermal Energy Conversion primer, Pacific International Center for High Technology Research (PICHTR) http://www.pichtr.org/mts_otec_published.pdf.
116 Small hydro: less than 10 MW. Mini-hydro: less than 500 KW. Micro-hydro: less than 100 KW. (Norms vary according to country).
117 IPCC 2007, WG3; *Mitigating Climate Change*, Contribution to the 4th assessment report of the IPCC.
118 www.aseanenergy.org/pressea/philippines/hydro/current.
119 *Quinze idées pour sauver le monde* (Fifteen ideas to save the world), Robert Socolow, planctpositivc.ch.
120 The rate expresses at the same time capitalism's preference for immediate gratification and its aversion to risk. The further in the future a return on an investment lies the more economists reduce its value in order to take into account 'the cost of time' and 'the cost of risk'. This depreciation is done by discounting, giving the current value of the investment or the cost. The current value being the basis of the discount, the rate is always positive. The closer it approaches integration, the less the depreciation. A critique of the ecological impact of this concept is proposed by René Passet in *L'economie et le vivant* (The economy and the living), Economica, Paris,1996 (2nd edition).
121 Simon Kyte, *The economics of climate change*, Current Issues Note 15, Greater London Authority, March 2007.
122 An organisation that provides Stock Exchange quotes.
123 The French Stock Exchange index.
124 European Commission, *A vision for PV technology for 2030 and beyond*, Preliminary Report by the PhotoVoltaic Technology Advisory Group, 2004.
125 http://www.ines-solaire.com/solpv/page1.html.
126 The kilowatt-hour, (kWh) is a unit of energy equal to 1000 watt hours or 3.6 megajoules. For constant power, energy in watt-hours is the product of power in watts and time in hours. The kilowatt-hour is most commonly known as a billing unit for energy delivered to consumers by electric utilities.
127 UNDP, *World energy assessment: energy and the challenge of sustainability*,

2000.
128 Translator's note: in English in the original.
129 IPCC, *Climate change 2007*, http://www.ipcc.ch/pdf/assessment-r.
130 *Energy technology perspective, scenarios and strategies to 2050*, Executive Summary, IEA, Paris, 2008,.
131 It may be objected in some quarters that the price could be increased gradually, but then we are again faced with the problem of the very short time that we have to stabilise the climate.
132 In France, the Constitutional Council rules on whether proposed statutes, after being adopted by Parliament, conform to the Constitution.
133 Stern Review (2006), p. 247.
134 Data from SIPRI, Stockholm.
135 The concept of 'energy system' is used here in the sense used by Barry Commoner, Jean-Paul Deléage et al; the energy system of a mode of production includes everything; its energy sources, converters, type of organisation (centralised or decentralised) and efficiency at different levels. In other words, the energy system is the mode of production considered from the point of view of energy. Barry Commoner, op. cit. Jean-Claude Debeir, Jean-Paul Deléage and Daniel Hemery, *Les servitudes de la puissance. Une histoire de l'energie* (The constraints of power. A history of energy), Flammarion, Paris, 1986.
136 In English in the original; emphasis in original.
137 According to the Commission's own data, the Directive on energy emissions from buildings would enable CO_2 emissions to be reduced by 82 million tonnes, while 398 million tonnes could be reduced by implementing the Directive to all buildings. *Proposal for a Directive of the European Parliament and of the Council on the energy performance of buildings*, COM (2001) 226 final.
138 Wolfram Krevitt, Uwe Klann, Stefan Kronshage, *Energy revolution. A sustainable pathway to a clean energy future for Europe*, Institute of Technical Thermodynamics (Stuttgart) & Greenpeace, Sept. 2005.
139 Esther Vivas, *Ne mange pas le monde: une autre agriculture pour un autre climat* (Don't eat the world: an alternative agriculture for another climate), http://www.europe-solidaire.org/spip.php?article15694
140 Curiously, the idea that climate change could be halted by a general mobilisation and adapting the process of production as the USA did during the Second World War has been advocated both by the Green lobbyist Lester Brown, *Plan B – for a global ecological pact*, Calman-Levy, Paris, 2007, and the militant Marxist Jonathan Neale, *Stop global warming. Change the world*, Bookmarks, London, 2008. This idea runs into a dead end because of the necessity of reducing production and transport of materials, and does not carry a serious enough warning against the danger of authoritarian solutions.
141 Intensity of the economy in energy, carbon or materials is used to designate the quantity of energy, carbon or materials needed to produce one unit of GDP.
142 Matthew Paterson, (2007), p. 225.
143 The flaw in this argument has been highlighted by L. Possoz and H. Jeanmart,

Comments on the electricity demand scenario in two studies from the DLR: MED-CSP & TRANS-CSP, ORMEE & MITEC engineering consultancy, Belgium (can be viewed online at', http://www.dlr.de/en/desktopdefault.aspx/).
144 *Financial Times*, London, 12 December 2007.
145 The choice of 1990 as a reference point is not fortuitous. The economic collapse of the Soviet Union and its buffer zones had transformed these countries into possessors of a volume of emission rights more or less corresponding to the reductions which the USA would have had to agree to if they had ratified the Protocol.
146 If all the signatories honour their commitments, EEA report No 8/2005, p.9, European Environment Agency, Copenhagen.
147 The Clean Development Mechanism (CDM) and the Joint Implementation Mechanism (JIM) are defined under the UNFCCC.
148 Cap-and-trade.
149 In the EU Emission Rights Exchange System, the penalty was 40 euros per tonne from 2005 – 2007, and has increased to 100 euros per tonne for the period 2008 – 2012.
150 The quota exchange had previously been implemented in the USA in the fight against lead in petrol, then in the fight against acid rain and against lead pollution. In no case can it be said that it was a remarkable success. On the subject of lead, see Curtis A. Moore 'Marketing Failure: the Experience With Air Pollution Trading in the US', *Health and Clean Air*, 2004. On the subject of acid rain, see Denny Ellerman et al. *'Emission trading under the US acid rain program'*, Centre for Energy and Environmental Research, MIT, *http://web.mit.edu/ceepr/www/napap.pdf*.
151 During the second period, 90% of quotas were distributed free.
152 Esso (£10 M), BP (£17.9 M), Shell (£20.7 M), according to Nick Davies, *The Guardian*, London, 2 June 2007.
153 This was the case for 18 universities in the UK, according to Nick Davies. The University of Manchester, for instance, had to pay £92,500 to buy emission rights. *The Guardian*, London, 2 June 2007.
154 At the end of lengthy discussions among specialists in the harmonisation of accounts, it was agreed that emission rights are not, strictly speaking, 'rights' to pollute. But these are well and truly 'assets', not simply 'financial instruments'. See Donald MacKenzie, *Making things the same: gases, emission rights and the politics of carbon markets*, University of Edinburgh, October 2007.
155 Press release from RWE: *RWE opposes statement of objections issued by German Federal Cartel Office: inclusion of CO_2 costs in the price of electricity no market manipulation'*, Essen, 12 October 2006.
156 *The Economist*, London, 9 September 2006.
157 Larry Lohman: 'Carbon trading. a critical conversation on climate change, privatisation and power', *Development Dialogue*, No.48, International Institute of Social Studies in The Hague, September 2006, http://www.thecornerhouse.org.uk.
158 Claire Stam, *Climat: un pas en avant, trois pas en arrière en Allemagne?* (Climate; one step forward, three steps back in Germany?), http://www.novethic.fr.

159 European Federation of Trade Unions, *The impact on employment of climate change and measures to reduce CO_2 emissions in the EU by 25% between now and 2030.* 11 July 2007. ULCOS (Ultra Low CO_2 steelmaking), a programme which receives 50% of its financial support from the EU.
160 In the case of the CDM, the term is CRE (Certified Reduction of Emissions), and URE (Units of Reduction of Emissions) in the case of the JIM.
161 *Proposal for a directive of the European Parliament and the Council of Europe, amending the directive 2003/87/EC, with the aim of improving and extending the ETS,* COM (2008)16 provisional. *Proposal for a decision by the European Parliament and the Council of Europe on the efforts of member states to reduce their emissions of greenhouse gases in order to meet their commitments to the reduction of greenhouse gases between now and 2020,* COM(2008)final.
162 The only limit is qualitative; carbon credit resulting from forestry projects are not considered equivalent to ETS rights.
163 See footnote 145.
164 Till Janzer and Jan Szyska, 'Profiting from pollution', *Finance New Europe* (on-line).
165 Antonio Gaspar, 'Steel industry should avoid 10 million tons of CO_2', *DiarioNet,* http://invertia.terra.com.br
166 Ibid. Using charcoal instead of coke in blast furnaces means the transformation of vast regions into 'green deserts' through planting gigantic monocultures of fast-growing trees such as eucalyptus. For this, Mittal has a special subsidiary, Arceol Mittal Brazil Forests.
167 In any case, CDM units of reduction must be certified, and the related expenses are the responsibility of the initiator of the project (who also chooses the certifying authority, which gives rise to considerable fraud and corruption.
168 *International Herald Tribune,* Paris, 3 July 2007.
169 *Africa, hardest hit by climate change, deserves greater share of carbon market benefits,* UNFCCC press release, 3/9/2008.
170 Aurélie Viellefosse, *Sector agreements in commitments post-2012,* French Ministry of Ecology and Sustainable Development, Department of Economic Studies and Environmental Evolution.
171 http://www.undp.org/content/undp/en/home.html.
172 AFP, Paris, 2 May 2007.
173 According to J-M Martin-Amouroux, (2008).
174 World Bank, '*State and Trends of the Carbon Market 2006* (update 1 January-30 September 2006)
175 http://www.noe21.org/docs/HFC23.htm.
176 A case similar to that of HFC-23 is that of the destruction of nitrous oxide in factories that produce nitric acid. See *CDM Watch, Newsletter No. 1,* Carbon Market Watch, Brussels.
177 Nick Davies, 'Truth about Kyoto: huge profits, little carbon saved', *The Guardian,* London, 2 June 2007.
178 M.W. Wara and D.G Victor, *A realistic policy on international carbon offsets,* Program on Energy and Sustainable Development, Working Paper 74, Stanford University, USA, April 2008.

179 In order to promote green electricity, governments have recourse either to a system of Green Certificates or one of feed-in-tariffs. http://www.ef4.be/fr/marche-energie/certificats-verts.
180 About 3,000 peak watts of solar panels. Peak Watts expresses the maximum power of a photovoltaic (PV) installation in standard conditions of hours of sunlight.
181 Launched with a great fanfare of publicity, the system functioned for less than one parliamentary term. Those who were the quickest to profit from it, because they had the means, evidently maintain their advantage ...
182 http://www.econologie.com/comparatif-energie-solaire-et-isolation-articles-3858.html.
183 The expression 'carbon leakage' is used to designate the danger of moving business with large volumes of carbon emission to countries which are not subject to reduction targets.
184 *Industry claims on carbon leakage exaggerated*, interview with Karsten Neuhoff on the site euractiv.com, 13 November 2008.
185 European Commission, *Questions and answers to the proposal to revise the ETS presented by the Commission,* Memo/08/35, 23 January 2008.
186 This also applies to the aviation companies, who are subject to a separate agreement; they will receive 90% of their quotas free, on the sole condition of ... putting a ceiling on their emissions.
187 *Emissions Trading Scheme – a step in the right direction,* Euractiv, Communiqué CEFIC, 15 December 2008.
188 Quoted by Benjamin Dessus, *L énergie, un défi planétaire* (Energy, a planetary challenge), Editions Belin, Paris, 1996.
189 The CDM is subject to a series of limitations; the most significant of these is that nuclear investments are not eligible.
190 REDD is the acronym for Reducing Emissions from Deforestation and Forest Degradation. Originally, only sustainable forestry practices were considered eligible to generate credits. REDD+ adds conservation.
191 An increasing number of droughts is hastening the death of trees, so that the forest is tending to absorb less carbon than it produces, which could turn it from a 'carbon sink' into a 'carbon source;', according to RAINFOR, a network of scientists making an inventory of Amazonian resources. 'Drought Sensitivity of the Amazon Rainforest', *Science,* 6 March 2009, Vol. 323, 1344-1347, quoted in a press release from INRA (French National Research Institute for Agriculture), 5 March 2009
192 Brown K., Boyd E., Corbera E. & Adger W.N., *How do CDM projects contribute to sustainable development,* Tyndall Centre for Climate Change Research, University of East Anglia, Norwich, June 2004.
193 Used during a conference and debate organised by Attac-Italia, Rome, 14 November 2009
194 Questions and Answers on the Commission's proposal to revise the EU Emissions Trading System, European Commission Memo 08/35, 23 January 2008.
195 Niklas Höhne and Christian Ellerman, *The EU s emission reduction target,*

intended use of CDM and its +2°C, Ecofys, September 2008, DG Internal policies of the EU, PE 408.552.
196 http://www.actu-environnement.com/ae/news/compromis_paquet_energie_climat_6398.php4.
197 Daniel Tanuro, *Bali Conference on Climate*, 2008, online at http://www.europe-solidaire.org.
198 One of these techniques is cultivation without ploughing, which Monsanto sees as an opportunity to increase the use of ROUND-UP.
199 George Monbiot, *the Guardian*, London, 26 June 2009.
200 The same tendencies apply to a large extent in Japan, an enthusiastic supporter of CDM.
201 *Business Week*, New York, 9 April 2001.
202 Can be seen on line at BarackObama.com.
203 This prognosis has meanwhile been confirmed by the Bangkok meeting in Autumn 2009, in the course of which the EU moved considerably closer to the US position, in particular in the attempt to avoid implementing the principle of common but differentiated responsibilities. See Christophe Aguiton, *Climat: de Bangkok à Copenhague* (Climate: from Bangkok to Copenhagen) http://www.europesolidaire.org/spip.php?article15448.
204 Immediately after Obama's election, BP and Shell made the spectacular announcement that they were abandoning a series of investments in wind-power in Europe, China, India and Turkey, so as to concentrate their capital in the USA, as the advantages promised by the new President allowed them to envisage higher returns on their investments. 'Blow to Brown as BP scraps British Renewable Plan to Focus on US', *The Guardian*, London, 7 November 2008.
205 *Plan to Make America a Global Energy Leader*, Barak Obama.
206 *US Coal Exports Seen as Target in Climate Fix*, Reuters, London, 8 October 2008, http://www.planetark.org/avantgo/dailynewsstory.cfm?newsid=50527.
207 *Us Biofuels Sector Sees Ally in Obama*, Reuters, 6 November 2008, http://planetark.org/avantgo/dailynewsstory.cfm?newsid=50947.
208 *Plan to Make America a Global Energy Leader*, Barack Obama.
209 'Second generation biofuels' refers to the production of ethanol from cellulose. 'Third generation' is a vague concept, covering all possible areas of research, including hydrogen-producing micro-organisms. EBI is the largest university research project ever funded by big business. The Institute is based at the University of California at Berkeley, and the researchers and their findings are generally at the disposal of BP.
210 Subsidies to farmers: 8.9 billion dollars in 2005. Tax concessions: 51 cents per gallon of ethanol.
211 *Folha di Sao Paolo*, Sao Paolo, 29 April 2007.
212 *Taking Stock of Climate Change*, EU Environment Department, 2002. http//www.europa.eu.int/comm/environment/ climat/climate_focus_fr.pdf
213 ECOTEC. *Analysis of the EU eco-industries, their employment and export potential*, Final Report on the Environment, 2002. http//www.europa.eu.int/comm/environment/enveco/industry_employment/ ecotec_exec_sum.pdf

214 European Commission; *Toward a Global Agreement on Climate Change at the Copenhagen Summit.*
215 *Solar technologies for producing electricity. Photovoltaic and solar thermodynamics in Germany; progress in research, methods of support and industrial perspectives.* Dossier from the Office for Science and Technology of the French Embassy in Germany, October 2008. Germany's price policy inspired supportive measures adopted in many countries, especially Belgium, which has already been quoted as an example.
216 A founder of the Nouveau Parti Anticapitaliste in France.
217 *Le Monde*, Paris, 5 September 2009.
218 René Riesel and Jaime Semprun, *Catastrophisme, administration du désastre et soumission durable*, (Catastrophism, disaster administration and sustainable submission). Editions. de l'Encyclopédie des Nuisances, Paris, 2008
219 Mark Lynas, *Six Degrees. Our Future on a Hotter Planet*, Fourth Estate, London, 2007.
220 44 billion dollars for the infrastructures, 40 billion for anti-poverty programmes, 2 billion to support anti-catastrophe measures. 'The fight against climate change; an imperative for human solidarity in a divided world', p. 194, *Global Report on Human Development, 2007-2008*, UNDP. The figure of 100 billion euros from 2020 was suggested at the preparatory discussions at the Copenhagen summit, December 2009.
221 UNDP (2007-2008).
222 http://www.iied.org/copenhagens-climate-finance-six-key-questions
223 *A Citizen's Guide to Climate Refugees*, Friends of the Earth Australia, 2005
224 Jean Pascal van Ypersele, 'L'injustice fondamentale des changements climatiques' (The fundamental injustice of climate change), in *Alternatives Sud, Vol. 13*, Louvain-la-Neuve, 2006
225 Jessica Azulay 'FEMA *planned to Leave New Orleans Poor Behind'*, http://newstandardnews.net
226 P. Le Tréhondat et P. Silberstein, *L'ouragan Katrina, le désastre annoncé*, Syllepse, Paris, 2005.
227 P. Schwartz and D. Randall, *An abrupt Climate Change Scenario and its Implications for US National Security*, Oct. 2003. This text has been published on several web pages, including Greenpeace. http://www.greenpeace.org/international/en/publications/reports/an-abrupt-climate-change-scena/
228 Bitter Division for Sierra Club on Immigration, *The New York Times*, 16 March 2004
229 http://www.unfpa.org/swp/2009/fr/index.shtml
230 *La Libre Belgique*, Brussels, 18 November 2009
231 Françoise Bartiaux and Jean-Pascal van Ypersele, 'The role of population growth in global warming', *International Population Conference, vol. 4*, p. 33-54, International Union for the Scientific Study of Population, Paris, 1993.
232 Contrary to what is claimed in the UN report, the IPCC does take it into account in its scenarios of human development.
233 *Le Soir*, Brussels, 30 November 2009.
234 *Anticipated indirect land use change associated with expanded use of biofuels and*

158   GREEN CAPITALISM: WHY IT CAN'T WORK

bioliquids in the EU – an analysis of the national renewable energy action plans, Institute European Environmental Policy, London, November 2010.
235   See for example, François Houtart, *L'Agroénergie – Solution pour le climat ou sortie de crise pour le capital?* Couleur Livres, Charleroi, 2009. (Agro-energy; climate solution or capitalist escape from crisis?)
236   In this context, see Ted Patzek's critique of the agreement between BP and the University of California at Berkeley about the creation of the Energy Bioscience Institute. http://www.stopbp-berkeley.org/CellulosicBiofuels.pdf
237   See the open letter from the World Rainforest Movement to the UNFCCC: http://209.85.229.132/search?q=cache:LEBhRJ0LU8sJ:www.wrm.org.uy/actors/CCC/Nairobi/Open_Letter.htm
238   *UN Convention Recognizes GM Trees Threat*, ISIS report, 30 May 2006, http://www.i-sis.org.uk/UNCRGETT.php
239   Mendel Biotechnology is collaborating with Monsanto and Bayer Crop Science. The company has recently announced the development of a partnership with BP in the biofuels sector. Less than three months previously, Mendel had acquired the largest collection in the world of Miscanthus seeds, a plant of great interest to BP and the EBI. Furthermore, in 2006, Monsanto and Mendel signed a 5-year agreement in which Monsanto was to develop the results of Mendel's research. http://www.berkeleydailyplanet.com
240   The first experiment with CCS on an industrial scale was carried out in the North Sea by the Norwegian firm Statoil, an important producer of natural gas. The gas from the Sleipnir deposit contains up to 9% of CO_2, significantly above the legal limit of 2.5%. As CO_2 emissions are taxed by the Norwegian government, since 1996 Statoil has been implementing the storage of a million tonnes of CO_2 per annum in a deep saline aquifer, located 800m beneath the ocean bottom. http://www.co2captureandstorage.info/co2db.php
241   *Special report; the capture and storage of carbon dioxide. Summary for decision makers*, p. 4, IPCC, 2005, http://www.ipcc.ch/pdf/special-reports/srccs/srccs_spm_ts_fr.pdf
242   Emissions of mercury vapours move very rapidly in the atmosphere, Increase of mercury pollution in developed countries where the standards of control are very strict could be attributed to the rise of the coal industry in Asia. Bernard Durand, *Energie et environnement. Les risques et les enjeux d'une crise annoncée*, Les Ulis, EDP Sciences, 2007. (Energy and Environment. The risks and stakes of a crisis foreseen).
243   http://news.bbc.co.uk/onthisday/hi/dates/stories/august/21/newsid_3380000/3380803.stm
244   http://recopol.nitg.tno.nl/
245   Richard Fisher, 'Climate Change may trigger earthquakes and volcanoes', *New Scientist*, London, 22 September 2009
246   Isabelle Stengers et Philippe Pignarre, *La sorcellerie capitaliste. Pratiques de désenvoûtement* (Capitalist witchcraft. Breaking the spell), La Découverte, Paris, 2004.
247   Four tonnes of water are needed to wash one tonne of coal. Transport of coal in the form of 'carboduc' requires about a tonne of water for every tonne of

crushed coal. As for the synthesis of liquid fuel from coal (achieved by the Nazis and by the apartheid regime in South Africa), this requires 1,500 litres of water per barrel of fuel.
248 Daniel Tanuro, *The Evidence from Fukushima: Nuclear Power Means Nuclear Catastrophe*, http://www.internationalviewpoint.org/spip.php?article2027
249 Storm Van Leeuwen, *Nuclear Power and Global Warming*, presentation at the seminar L'énergie nucléaire au 21ᵉ siècle, Brussels, 19 October 2006
250 Benjamin Dessus and Hélène Gassin, *So Watt? L'énergie, une affaire de citoyens* (So Watt? Energy, the business of citizens), Editions de l'Aube, La Tour d'Aigues, France, 2006.
251 This limit could be increased by opting for plutonium reactors, but in this case, there would evidently be a major danger of military proliferation.
252 *Energy Technology Perspectives*, quoted from the french version *Perspectives des technologies de l'énergie. Au service du plan d'action du G8. Scénarios et stratégies à l'horizon 2050*, AIE, Paris, 2008
253 France has particularly distinguished itself in the person of Claude Allègre and his colleague Vincent Courtillot. In his relentless determination to prove that global warming is natural, Courtillot has almost gone so far as to forget that the earth is round. The scathing response from the climatologist Edouard Bard (*The Knights of the Flat Earth*) can be found on line at this excellent site: http://www.realclimate.org
254 Stern Review, (2006), p. 325.
255 Blinded by the criterion of cost-efficiency, the designers of the EU emission rights market (ETS) did not even realise that this was qualitatively different from the US market in rights of sulphur gas (SOx) emission, which they used as a model. Now, the elimination of SOx, which causes acid rain, is above all a technical problem and, if the worst comes to the worst, all methods are good. It matters little whether the right to emit a tonne of sulphur derives from the implementation of procedure A or procedure B. But it is not the same in the case of fossil CO_2, as temporary absorption by a sink is not equivalent to the structural suppression of a source.
256 Carbon Tracker Initiative, 'Unburnable carbon – are the world's financial markets carrying a carbon bubble?', http://www.carbontracker.org/carbonbubble.
257 *The Guardian*, London, 15 July 2011
258 *The Guardian*, London, 12 July 2011.
259 It was not for love of metaphors that Marx wrote in *Capital* that one day 'the right of some individuals over some parts of the earth will seem as absurd as the right of one person to own another', but because the absurdity is the same in both cases; appropriation of natural resources, the essential identity between 'the natural power of humanity' and 'the natural power of the Earth' was repeated several times in *Capital* and in *the Theories Of Surplus Value*; the labour force is a natural resource. This may appear to contradict the celebrated assertion that capitalism ruins 'the only true sources of wealth – the earth and the worker', which implies two different sources. But the contradiction is more apparent than real. In the first instance, Marx is using the perspective of

160   GREEN CAPITALISM: WHY IT CAN'T WORK

thermodynamics – the ability of living beings to act as energy converters. In the second, he is approaching the question from the point of view of created wealth – a field in which human production is obviously distinguished from natural production by its social nature and the use of tools. The labour force is thus perceived as a double reality. On the one hand as a natural resource ('all work is ultimately the use of human muscles, nerves and brains'), on the other as a social resource created by cooperation between producers and by the development of knowledge.

260 Marx, *Capital*, Vol. 3
261 The pseudo-scientific mystification which often characterises these estimates cannot be too strongly denounced. In the US, for example, all policies of environmental regulation have to be justified by a cost-benefit analysis. The calculations are reached by mathematical models based on hypotheses. These are not generally made explicit, and in some cases are kept secret. The World Resources Institute has revealed that the US administration uses a model based largely on the hypothesis that a rise in temperature of 17°C would have no significant impact on agricultural production. http://www.wri.org/stories/2011/07/social-cost-carbon-and-climate-change-policy?utm_campaign=wridigest&utm_medium=email&utm_source=wridigest-2011-07&utm_content=hyperlink&utm_term=SocialCostofCarbonAndClimateChangePolicy-FullStory
262 There are other examples, however. Thus, the fight against the destruction of the ozone layer is led by a simple regulatory measure – the phasing out of CFCs. This is proving successful, as the emissions have been reduced by 80% since the signing of the Montreal Protocol in 1987. Certainly, the phasing out of fossil fuels is more complicated than the phasing out of CFCs, but nevertheless it is not impossible.
263 Ernest Mandel, *Late Capitalism*, New Left Books, London, 1975.
264 Jean-Marie Chevalier *Les grandes batailles de l'énergie* (The big battles for energy), Gallimard, 2004.
265 This possibility is explicitly mentioned by Nicholas Stern (2006).
266 Daniel J. Weiss et Alexandra Kougentakis, '*Big Oil Misers*', 2009, http://www.americanprogress.org/
267 Damian Carrington and Stefano Valentino, 'Bio fuels boom in Africa as British firms lead rush on land for plantations', *The Guardian*, London, 31 May 2011.
268 WWF France: '-30% de CO_2 = 684.000 emplois. L'équation gagnante pour la France', www.wwf.fr/content/download/4064/20989/version/1/file/EMPLOI+CLIMAT+BD_1.pdf.
269 This chauvinism is present in the subtitle of the study – 'the winning equation for France'.
270 Indian ecologist.
271 Anil Agarwal and Sunita Nairin, '*The Atmospheric Rights of All People on Earth*', www.cseindia.org. The scenario 'contraction and convergence' is advocated by the Global Commons Institute http://www.gci.org.uk.
272 The expression 'semi-permanent property rights over the air' is used by David Victor in his '*The collapse of the Kyoto Protocol and the struggle to slow global*

warming', Princeton University Press, New Jersey, 2001
273 Contribution by Claude Serfati and François Chesnais in *'Capital contre nature'*, JM Harribey and M. Löwy, PUF, Paris, 2003.
274 Centre d'Information et d'Analyse sur le Dioxyde de Carbone, http://cdiac.ornl.gov/.
275 Ernest Mandel, *Long waves of capitalist development. A Marxist Interpretation*, Verso, London, 1995
276 Michel Husson, 'Le capitalisme toxique', *Inprécor*, Paris, No. 541-542, http://hussonet.free.fr/.
277 In the US, the long wave of expansion began in 1940. In Europe, it did not get off the ground until 1947.
278 From this point of view, neo-liberalism is more than a policy: it is the contemporary, decadent form of appropriation of surplus value by the ruling class. This goes some way to explaining why common-sense solutions such as nationalisation of energy and some planning are not even considered, although they are not in themselves anti-capitalist.
279 *Le Monde*, Paris, 3 December 2008.
280 The expression 'destructive forces' was used by Marx and Engels in *The German Ideology*.
281 Isabelle Stengers, *Au temps des catastrophes – Résister à la barbarie qui vient* (In the times of catastrophes – Resist the coming barbarism), La Découverte, Paris, 2009.
282 Marcel Mazoyer and Laurence Roudart, *Histoire des agricultures du monde* (History of world agriculture), 1997.
283 Mike Davis, *Late Victorian holocausts, El Niño famines and the making of the Third World*, Verso, London, 2002.
284 Michel Husson, *Un pur capitalisme*, Page Deux, Lausanne, 2008.
285 Hans Jonas, *The imperative of responsibility: in search of ethics for the technological age*, University of Chicago Press, Illinois,1984.
286 This point of view implies that technology is neutral, independent of modes of production, which paradoxically brings Jonas closer to the theoreticians of 'real socialism'.
287 Hans Jonas, (1984), p. 155.
288 See D. Tanuro *'Home': écologie religion ou écologie de combat?* ('Home': a religion of ecology or a religion of struggle), on line at http://www.europe-solidaire.org/spip.php?article14887.
289 Jared Diamond, (1984), p. 491. For a critique of this bewildering theory, see Daniel Tanuro, *'Le plafond photosynthétique n'est pas près de nous tomber sur la tête'* (The photosynthetic ceiling is not about to fall on our heads), *Le Grand Soir*, 12 September 2007 http://www.legrandsoir.info/. Vitousek et al. 'Human Domination on Earth's Ecosystems', *Science*, vol. 277, Washington DC, 25 July 2007.
290 Jacques Grinevald for instance. There is a recording of a public debate with the present writer, Geneva, 4 April 2009. http://www.solidarites.ch/geneve/index.php/videos/183-audio-decroissance-etou-ecosocialisme-jacques-grinevald-et-daniel-tanuro.

291 Garret Hardin, 'The Tragedy of the Commons', *Science*, Washington DC, 13 December 1968, Vol. 162, No.3859, pp. 1243-1248.
292 Figures from the Carbon Dioxyde Analysis Information Centre.
293 Author's note: because the capitalist monopolises the surplus value.
294 Author's note: because the capitalist doesn't want to spend, but to invest.
295 Karl Marx, *Theories of surplus value*, Vol. 1. The bad conscience referred to here ironically by Marx goes some way towards explaining the enthusiasm for the theories of Jonas and his colleagues, which coincide precisely with a phase of capitalism in which the blocking of the system is partly caused by conspicuous luxury consumption. This also explains the success among the wealthier echelons of society of conscience-salving goods such as hybrid vehicles and photovoltaic panels.
296 'Life in a land without growth', *New Scientist*, London, 15 October 2008.
297 This drift has not escaped the notice of some of his former friends; see *Cahiers de l'IEESDS*, No.2, May 2008 (Institut des Études Economiques et Sociales pour la Décroissance Soutenable).
298 Serge Latouche, *Survivre au développement*, (Surviving Development), Mille et une Nuits, Paris, 2004.
299 Serge Latouche, (2004).
300 See for example Paul Ariès 'Pour un rationnement désirable' (For a desirable rationing), *Journal La Décroissance*, No.50, Lyon, June 2008.
301 Hervé Kempf, *Pour sauver la planète, sortez du capitalisme,* (Leave capitalism to save the planet), Editions du Seuil, Paris, 2009.
302 Quoted in Karl Kautsky, *La question agraire. Etude sur les tendances de l'agriculture moderne* (The agrarian question. Study of the tendencies of modern agriculture), Giard & Brière, Paris 1900, facsimilé reprint by F.Maspéro, Paris, 1970.
303 Nicholas Georgescu-Roegen, *La décroissance. Entropie, écologie, économie,* Sang de la Terre, 1979. There is an interesting critique of this author's theories of thermodynamics by Pierre Gillis and Grégoire Wallenborn in *Les Cahiers Marxistes,* Brussels, No.235, May-June 2007.
304 Daniel Tanuro, 'Marx, Mandel et les limites naturelles' in *Contretemps*, No.20, Paris, October. 2007.
305 Marx states categorically that all human development is inevitable enclosed within two limits; 'the fecundity of nature, which constitutes one limit, a point of departure, and the development of the productive force of nature, which constitutes the other'. *Capital,* Vol. 3, Ch.37.
306 Marx mentions the global textile trade as one of the causes of the impoverishment of the soil under capitalism. He does not draw the conclusion from this that a partial decentralisation of agricultural production is necessary, but this is consistent with his condemnation of the separation between town and country.
307 It is superior to James Lovelock's GAIA hypothesis, whether, whether under a 'weak' or 'strong' form, does not take the social mode of production into account.
308 Barry Commoner *The closing circle; nature, man and technology*, Knopf, New

York, 1971.
309 John Bellamy. Foster, *Marx's ecology; materialism and nature*, Monthly Review Press, New York, 2000. John Bellamy Foster and Paul Burkett, Ecological Economics and Classical Marxism, *Organization & Environment*, Vol. 17, No.1, 32-60.
310 For instance, in discussing the situation of the emerging working classes before the Industrial Revolution, Marx notes that 'since the technological mode of production did not yet have a specifically capitalist character, the subordination of labour to capital was not yet complete', *Capital*, Vol.1, Ch. 28.
311 V.I. Lenin, *The agrarian question and the 'critics of Marx'*, Chap. IV, 1901.
312 Nicholai Bukharin, *Historical materialism, a system of sociology*, 1921.
313 Ernest Mandel, 'La dialectique de la croissance. A propos du rapport Mansholt' (Dialectics of growth and the Mansholt report), in *Mai*, Brussels, Nov-Dec. 1972.
314 Ernest Mandel, 'Ten theses on the social and economic laws governing the society transitional between capitalism and socialism', *Critique*, No.3, Autumn 1974.
315 Michaël Löwy, *'Progrès destructif: Marx, Engels et l'écologie'* (Destructive progress: Marx, Engels and ecology), on line at http://acc.agora.eu.org/Progres-destructif-Marx-Engels-et-l-ecologie.html.
316 Joël Kovel and Michaël Löwy 'An ecosocialist manifesto', http://www.europe-solidaire.org/spip.php?article2278.
317 William Morris, *Art and socialism*, http://www.marxists.org/archive/morris/works/1884/as/as.htm

About Resistance Books and the IIRE

Resistance Books

Resistance Books is the publishing arm of Socialist Resistance, a revolutionary Marxist organisation which is the British section of the Fourth International. Resistance Books publishes books jointly with the International Institute for Research and Education in Amsterdam and independently.

Further information about Resistance Books, including a full list of titles currently available and how to purchase them, can be obtained at http://www.resistancebooks.org, or by writing to Resistance Books, PO Box 62732, London, SW2 9GQ.

Socialist Resistance is an organisation active in the trade union movement and in many campaigns against imperialist intervention in places like Afghanistan or Iraq, in solidarity with Palestine and with anti-capitalist movements across the globe. We are ecosocialist – we argue that much of what is produced under capitalism is socially useless and either redundant or directly harmful. Capitalism's drive for profit is creating environmental disaster – and it is the poor, the working class and people in the Global South who are paying the highest price for this.

We have been long-standing supporters of women's liberation and the struggles of lesbians, gay people, bisexuals and transgender people. We believe these struggles must be led by those directly affected – none so fit to break the chains as those who wear them. We work in anti-racist and anti-fascist networks, including campaigns for the rights of immigrants and asylum seekers.

Socialist Resistance believes that democracy is an essential component of any successful movement of resistance and struggle. With Britain and the western imperialist countries moving into a long period of capitalist austerity and crisis, deeper than any since the Second World War, Socialist Resistance stands together with all those who are organising to make another world possible.

Socialist Resistance is the bi-monthly magazine of the organisation, which can be read online at www.socialistresistance.org. Socialist Resistance can be contacted by email at contact@socialistresistance.org or by post at PO Box 62732, London, SW2 9GQ.

International Viewpoint is the English language online magazine of the Fourth International which can be read online at www.internationalviewpoint.org.

The International Institute for Research and Education

The International Institute for Research and Education (IIRE) is an international foundation, recognised in Belgium as an international scientific association by a Royal decree of 11th June 1981. The IIRE provides activists and scholars worldwide with opportunities for research and education in three locations: Amsterdam, Islamabad and Manila.

Since 1982, when the Institute opened in Amsterdam, its main activity has been the organisation of courses in the service of progressive forces around the world. Our seminars and study groups deal with all subjects related to the emancipation of the world's oppressed and exploited. It has welcomed hundreds of participants from every inhabited continent. Most participants have come from the Third World.

The IIRE has become a prominent centre for the development of critical thought and interaction, and the exchange of experiences, between people who are engaged in daily struggles on the ground. The Institute's sessions give participants a unique opportunity to step aside from the pressure of daily activism. The IIRE gives them time to study, reflect upon their involvement in a changing world and exchange ideas with people from other countries.

Our website is constantly being expanded and updated with freely downloadable publications, in several languages, and audio files. Recordings of several recent lectures given at the institute can be downloaded from www.iire.org - as can talks given by founding Fellows such as Ernest Mandel and Livio Maitan, dating back to the early 1980s.

The IIRE publishes *Notebooks for Study and Research* to focus on themes of contemporary debate or historical or theoretical importance. Lectures and study materials given in sessions in our Institute, located in Amsterdam, Manila and Islamabad, are made available to the public in large part through the Notebooks.

Different issues of the Notebooks have also appeared in languages besides English and French, including German, Dutch, Arabic, Spanish, Japanese, Korean, Portuguese, Turkish, Swedish, Danish and Russian.

For a full list of the *Notebooks for Study and Research*, visit http://bit.ly/IIRENSR or subscribe online at: http://bit.ly/NSRsub. To order the *Notebooks*, email iire@iire.org or write to International Institute for Research and Education, Lombokstraat 40, Amsterdam, NL-1094.